A Daybook for August

in Yellow Springs, Ohio

A Memoir in Nature

and a Handbook for August,
Being a Personal Narrative and Synthesis of
Common Events in Nature
between 1981 and 2018
in Southwestern Ohio, with Applications
for the Lower Midwest and Middle Atlantic
Region, Containing Weather Guidelines
and a Variety of Natural Calendars,
Reflections by the Author
and Seasonal Quotations
from Ancient and Modern Writers

By

Bill Felker

A Daybook for the Year in Yellow Springs, Ohio

Volume 8: August

Cover from a watercolor by Libby Rudolph

Copyright 2018 by Bill Felker

Published by The Green Thrush Press
P.O. Box 431, Yellow Springs, Ohio
Printed in the United States of America
Charleston, SC
July 2018

All rights reserved, including the right to reproduce this book or portions thereof in any form whatsoever.
ISBN-13: 978-1720691921
ISBN-10: 1720691924

For my mother and father

No one suspects the days to be gods.

Ralph Waldo Emerson

Introduction

Here are no stories told you of what is to be seen at the other end of the world, but of things at home, in your own Native Countrey, at your own doors, easily examinable with little travel, less cost, and very little hazard. This book doth not shew you a Telescope, but a Mirror, it goes not about to put a delightful cheat upon you, with objects at a great distance, but shews you yourselves.

Joshua Childrey, 1660

The Daybook Format

The format of my notes in this daybook owes more than a little to the almanacs I wrote for the *Yellow Springs News* between 1984 and 2018. The use of quotations, daily statistics, the weather outlooks, the seasonal calendar, and the daybook journal were and still are part of my regular routine of collecting and organizing impressions about the place in which I live.

Setting: The principal habitat described here is that of Glen Helen, a preserve of woods and glades that lies on the eastern border of the village of Yellow Springs in southwestern Ohio. At its northern edge, the Glen joins with John Bryan State Park to form a corridor about ten miles long and half a mile wide along the Little Miami River. The north section of the Glen Helen /John Bryan complex is hilly and heavily wooded and is the best location for spring wildflowers. The southern portion, "South Glen" as it is usually called, is a combination of open fields, wetlands, and wooded flatlands. Here I found many flowers and grasses of summer and fall. Together, the two Glens and John Bryan Park provide a remarkable cross section of the fauna and flora of the eastern United States.

Other habitats in the daybook journal include my yard with its several small gardens; the village of Yellow Springs itself, a town of about 4,000 at the far eastern border of the Dayton suburbs; the Caesar Creek Reservoir twenty miles south of Yellow Springs. My trips away from that environment were principally northeast to Chicago, Madison, Wisconsin and northern Minnesota, east to Washington and New York, southeast to the Carolinas and Florida, southwest to Arkansas, Louisiana and Texas, and occasionally through the Southwest to California and the Northwest, two excursions to Belize in Central America, several to Italy.

Quotations: The passages from ancient and modern writers (and sometimes from my alter egos) which accompany each day's notations are lessons from my readings, as well as from distant seminary and university training, here put to work in service of the reconstruction of my sense of time and space. They are a collection of reminders, hopes, and promises for me that I find implicit in the seasons. They have become a kind of a cosmological scrapbook for me and the philosophical underpinning of this narrative.

Astronomical Data: The *Daybook* includes approximate dates for astronomical events, such as star positions, meteor showers, solstice, equinox, perihelion (the Sun's position closest to Earth), and aphelion (the Sun's position farthest from Earth).

I have included the sunrise and sunset for Yellow Springs as a general guide to the progression of the year in this location, but those statistics also reflect trends that are world wide, if more rapid in some places and slower in others.

Even though the day's length is almost never exactly the same from one town to the next, a minute gained or lost in Yellow Springs is often a minute lost or gained elsewhere, and the Yellow Springs numbers can be used as a simple way of watching the lengthening or shortening of the days, and, therefore, of watching the turn of the planet. For those who wish to keep track of the Sun themselves in their own location, abundant sources are now available for this information in local and national media.

Average Temperatures: Average temperatures in Yellow Springs are also part of each day's entry. Since the rise and fall of temperatures in other parts of the North America, even though they may start from colder or warmer readings, keep pace with the temperatures here, the highs and lows in Yellow Springs are, like solar statistics, helpful indicators of the steady progress of the year throughout most of the states along the 40th Parallel (except in the mountains). The daybook journal entries can be cross-referenced with the list of monthly average temperatures between 1981 and 2017 in order to compare the daily inventories with the month's weather in a given year.

Weather: My daily, weekly and monthly weather summaries have been distilled from over thirty years of observations. They are descriptions of the local weather history I have kept in order to track the gradual change in temperature, precipitation and cloud cover through the year. I have also used them in order to try to identify particular characteristics of each day. They are not meant to be predictions.

Although my interest in the Yellow Springs microclimate at first seemed too narrow to be of use to those who lived outside the area, I began to modify it to meet the needs of a number of regional and national farm publications for which I started writing in the mid 1980s. And so, while the summaries are based on my records in southwestern Ohio, they can be and have been used, with interpretation and interpolation, throughout the Lower Midwest, the Middle Atlantic States and the East.

The Natural Calendar: In this section, I note the progress of foliage and floral changes, farm and garden practices, migration times for common birds and peak periods of insect activity. Some of these notes are second hand; I'm a sky watcher, but not an astronomer, and I rely on the government's astronomical data and a few other references for much of my information about the stars and the sun. I am also a complete amateur at bird watching, and most of the migration dates used in the seasonal calendar come from published sources. And even though I keep close track of the farm year, the percentages listed for planting and harvesting are interpretations of averages supplied by the state's weekly crop reports.

At the beginning of each spring and summer month, I have included a floating calendar of blooming dates which lists approximate flowering times for many plants, shrubs and trees in an average Ohio Valley season. The floating chronology describes the relationship between events more than exact dates of these occurrences.

Although the flora of the eastern and central United States is hardly limited to the species mentioned here, the flowers listed are common enough to provide easily recognized landmarks for gauging the advance of the year. I found, for example, that a record of my drives south during April complemented the floating calendar and allowed me to see the approximate differences between Yellow Springs and other locations. I also learned that April in the Lower Midwest is more like March in the Southeast and more like May in the Upper Midwest. The Natural Calendar summaries, then, provide guidelines for moveable feasts that shift not only according to fixed geographical regions but also according to the weather in any particular year.

Daybook Entries: The journal entries in the daybook section provide the raw material from which I wrote the Natural Calendar digests. They offer a record that anyone with a few guidebooks could make, and they include just a small number of the natural markers that anyone might discover.

When I began to take notes about the world around me, I found that there were few descriptions of actual events in nature available for southwestern Ohio. There was no roadmap for the course of the year. My daily observations, as narrow and incomplete as they were, were especially significant to me since I had found no other narrative of the days, no other depiction of what was actually occurring around me. In time, the world came into focus with each particle I named. I saw concretely that time and space were the sum of their parts.

As my notes for each day accumulated, I could see the wide variation of events that occurred from year to year; at the same time, I saw a unity in this syncopation from which I could identify numerous sub-seasons and with which I could understand better the kind of habitat in which I was living and, consequently, myself.

When I paged through the journal entries for each day, I was drawn back to the space in which they were made. I browsed and imagined, returned to the journey.

Companions: Many friends, acquaintances and family members have contributed their observations to the daybook, and their participation has taught me that my private seasons are also community seasons, and that all of our experiences together help to lay the foundation for a rich, local consciousness.

The Month of August
August Averages: 1981 through 2018
Normal August Average Temperature: 72.7

Year	Average
1981	72.8
1982	70.7
1983	75.8
1984	71.5
1985	70.8
1986	69.8
1987	73.2
1988	77.2
1989	72.2
1990	71.6
1991	73.7
1992	68.9
1993	75.1
1994	71.7
1995	78.0
1996	73.2
1997	69.8
1998	74.2
1999	71.3
2000	71.1
2001	73.5
2002	75.8
2003	73.0
2004	69.0
2005	74.9
2006	73.7
2007	76.9
2008	71.4
2009	71.0
2010	75.8
2011	73.9
2012	73.0
2013	72.8
2014	73.9
2015	70.7
2016	76.8
2017	70.7
2018	74.8

August 1st
The 213th Day of the Year

Take Stock in August,
Count your Days.
Measure the Harvest,
The Hours of Sunlight.

Celtus

Sunrise/set: 5:33/7:49
Day's Length: 14 hours 16 minutes
Average High/Low: 85/64
Average Temperature: 75
Record High: 96 – 1935
Record Low: 52 – 1895

Weather
Today is usually in the 80s, with a 15 percent chance of an afternoon in the 70s, and 20 percent for 90s. The sun shines on at least 85 percent of the days, and the chance of rain is 25 percent. Cool lows in the 50s occur one or two nights in a decade.

The Weather in the Week Ahead
The Dog Days ordinarily continue this week of the year, the daily possibility of highs in the 80s and 90s remaining near July levels. However, August 3rd, 4th, and 5th are the last days of the summer on which there is a 40 percent chance of highs in the 90s, and chances of highs in the 80s are steady at around 50 percent. Cool days do occur 15 to 25 percent of the years, and afternoons only in the 60s are occasionally recorded between August 2nd and 11th. Morning lows are typically in the 60s, although one fourth of the nights carry temperatures in the middle 50s.

The August Outlook
Six thunderstorms usually occur in August. They are most likely to occur on the hot afternoons between the 1st and the 11th.

Total average precipitation is near three inches in the Yellow Springs area, a little less than in July. The days with the most precipitation are August 4th, 5th, 10th, 11th, 18th, 19th, 21st, and 28th. The driest days in my weather history: August 9th, 12th, 13th, 14th, and 22nd.

Nights grow about an hour and ten minutes longer by the end of the month along the 40th Parallel. The first week loses two minutes every day; by the last week, the loss is up to three minutes every 24 hours. Even though the length of the day shortens, the percentage of possible sunshine per day increases to near 80 percent, the highest of the Ohio year.

The eighth month typically brings ten completely sunny days and up to two weeks of partly cloudy weather. The brightest August days, those with better than an 80 percent chance of sun, are the 1st, 2nd, 8th, 9th, 12th, 13th, 25th, and 26th. Totally cloudy days are rare; the 18th, the 23rd and the 28th are the only days on which the chances of overcast conditions reach 50 percent.

Normal average temperatures decline from the mid 70s to the lower 70s all across the region. Highs fall from their peak of 85 at the rate of about one degree every week, reaching 81 by the first of September. Average lows drop from 64 to 60.

The August days most likely to bring milder temperatures (highs below 80 degrees) occur in the second half of the month: the 20th, 23rd, 24th, 29th, and 30th. The hottest days, those most likely to bring 90s or above, generally come at the beginning of the month. Adding to the warmth, August's wind speed is the lowest of the year, and humidity is the highest, an average of about 80 percent after sundown. Chances of oppressive heat gradually fall from 35 percent between the 1st and the 4th down to 15 percent by the end of the month.

Estimated Pollen Count

On a scale of 0 - 700 grains per cubic meter: Most of the pollen in the air this month comes from ragweed.

August 1: 35	August 5: 40
August 10: 50	August 15: 85
August 20: 160	August 25: 200
August 30: 300	

Estimated Mold Count
On a scale of 0 - 7,000 grains per cubic meter:

August 1: 4000
August 10: 6000
August 20: 4800
August 30: 5500

August 5: 4800
August 15: 4000
August 25: 5100

Summercount

Between the last week of May through the first week of September, the fourteen major cool fronts of summer cross the United States. As these high-pressure systems approach, temperatures and humidity typically rise. After the passage of the fronts, slightly cooler weather occurs, suitable for outdoor work and recreation, followed by up to a week of heat and humid conditions. August fronts often reach the Mississippi around the following dates; they come through about two days earlier in the West, a day or two later in the East.

August 4: The weather in advance of this minor front is some of the hottest of the summer. Highs in the cool 70s and lows in the 50s are rare in most of the nation between August 1st and 3rd. Rain very often accompanies the August 4th front (the day of the front's arrival brings showers more often than any day since the first week of July), but after the system moves east, the likelihood for highs in the 90s begins a steady decline, and the possibility for a high only in the 60s appears on the horizon of possibility. Rainfall remains light and clouds infrequent through the 9th, which is usually one of the sunniest and driest days of the summer.

August 10: The August 10th cool front can bring frost to the higher elevations in the West. Its strength also frequently causes violent weather throughout the Great Plains and the South. This second August front also contributes to the erosion of chances of highs in the 90s. The likelihood of rain increases sharply for two to three days because of this weather system, and within the next seven days along the 40th Parallel, lows reach into the 40s fifteen times more often than they do during the first week of August.

August 17: This is the weather system that brings the chance of a killing frost to portions of the North; snow occurs at upper elevations in the Rocky Mountains.

August 24: This high erodes summer a little more, often bringing an end to the Dog Days. At average elevations along the 40th Parallel, odds for an afternoon in the 90s are now only half of what they were two weeks ago, and the likelihood of mild highs only in the 70s is twice as great as it was at the end of July. As this cool front moves away, the period between August 25 and August 27 usually brings a return of warmer temperatures in the 80s or 90s.

August 29: Rain precedes this front two years in three, and when the August 29 high-pressure system arrives, the likelihood for chilly highs only the 60s or 70s becomes almost autumnal. August 30 is typically the coldest day of the month, and it brings a 50 percent chance of a high just in the 70s along the 40th Parallel, the first time chances of that have been so good since the end of June. Nights in the 40s or 50s continue to occur half the time, and the morning of the 29th brings the slight possibility (a five percent chance) of light frost to the lower Midwest for first time since the beginning of early summer.

Key to the Nation's Weather

The typical August temperature at average elevations along the 40th Parallel, the average of the high of 83 and the low of 63, is 73 degrees. Using the following chart based on weather statistics from around the country, one can calculate approximate temperatures in other locations close to the cities listed.

For example, with the base of 73 you can estimate normal temperatures in Minneapolis by subtracting 3 degrees from the base average. Or add 5 degrees to find out the likely conditions in Atlanta during the month.

Fairbanks AK	-18
Seattle, WA	-9
Cheyenne WY	-7
Portland, ME	-6

Minneapolis MN	-3
AVERAGE ALONG THE 40TH PARALLEL:	73
Washington D.C.	+2
St. Louis MO	+5
Atlanta GA	+5
Little Rock AR	+7
New Orleans LA	+9
Miami FL	+9

A Floating Sequence
For the Blooming of Wildflowers and Perennials

The following list is based on my personal observations in southwestern Ohio over a period of 30 years. The dates are approximate, but I have tried to show a relatively true sequence of first blossoming times during an average year. Although the dates on all flower calendars are somewhat arbitrary (and may vary by up to 30 days between the Canadian border and the South in Late Summer), a "floating calendar" can be used throughout the country by adjusting (floating) the sequence to fit the climate and the particular year.

July 16:	Butterfly Bush (*Buddleja davidii*)
July 17:	Tick Trefoil (*Desmodium canadense*)
July 18:	Velvet Leaf (*Abutilon theophrasti*)
	Bull Thistle (*Cirsium vulgare*)
July 19:	Water Hemlock (*Cicuta maculate*)
	Early Goldenrod (*Solidago*)
July 20:	Resurrection Lily (*Lycoris squamigera*)
July 21:	Burdock (*Arctium lappa*)
July 22:	Ironweed (*Vernonia gigantean*)
	Monkey Flower (*Mimulus guttatus*)
	Arrowhead (*Sagittaria latifolia*)
July 23:	Stonecrop Autumn Joy Sedum (*Sedum telephium*)
	Joe Pye Weed (*Eutrochium purpureum*)
July 23:	Turk's Cap Lily (*Lilium superbium*)
	Jimson Weed (*Datura stramonium*)
July 24:	Field Thistle (*Cirsium arvense*)
	Common Ragweed (*Ambrosia artemisiifolia*)

July 25:	Tall Coneflower (*Rudbeckia laciniata*)
	Narrow-Leaved Mountain Mint (*Pycnanthemum tenuifolium*)
July 27:	Biennial Gaura (*Gaura biennis*)
July 28:	White Snakeroot (*Ageratina altissima*)
July 29:	Clearweed (*Pilea pumila*)
July 30:	Jumpseed (*Persicaria virginiana*)
July 31:	Boneset (*Eupatorium perfoliatum*)
	Pigweed (*Amaranthus palmeri*)
August 1:	Mad-Dog Skullcap (*Scutellaria lateriflora*)
	Giant Yellow Hyssop (*Agastache nepetoides*)
August 2:	Prickly Mallow (*Sida spinosa*)
	Great Ragweed (*Ambrosia trifida*)
August 3:	Milk Purslane (*Euphorbia maculate*)
August 4:	Willow Herb (*Epilobium angustifolium)*
August 5:	Japanese Knotweed (*Fallopian japonica*)
August 7:	Love Vine (*Cassytha filiformis*)
August 8:	False Boneset (*Brickellia eupatoriodes*)
August 9:	Bur Cucumber (*Cucumis anguria*)
August 10:	Three-Seeded Mercury (*Acalypha rhomboidea*)
August 11:	Water Horehound (*Lycopus americanus*)
August 12:	Tall Goldenrod (*Solidago altissima*)
August 14:	Great Blue Lobelia (*Lobelia siphilitica*)
August 16:	Rose Pink (*Glandularia canadensis*)
August 23:	Hog Peanut (*Amphicarpaea bracteata*)
August 24:	Jerusalem Artichoke (*Helianthus tuberosus*)
August 29:	Beggarticks (*Bidens pilosa* or *frondosa*)
August 30:	Bur Marigold (*Bidens tripartite*)
August 31:	Heath Aster (S*ymphyotrichum ericoides*)
September 1:	New England Aster (*Symphyotrichum novae-angliae*)
September 8:	Zigzag Goldenrod (*Solidago flexicaulis*)
September 9:	Small White Aster (*Symphyotrichum ericoides*)
	Heart-Leafed Aster (*Symphyotrichum cordifolium*)
September 10:	Panicled Aster (*Symphyotrichum lanceolatum*)

August Phenology

When honeysuckle berries ripen and hickory nuts and black walnuts drop into the undergrowth, then gardeners dig their potatoes.

When robins make their clucking migration calls, then farmers make corrective lime and fertilizer applications for August and September seeding.

When green acorns fall to the sweet rocket growing back for next year's flowers, then black walnut trees have lost about a third of their leaves and hummingbirds, wood ducks, Baltimore orioles and purple martins start to disappear south.

When the violet Joe Pye weed flowers become gray like the thistledown, then peaches, processing tomatoes and peppers are almost all picked along the 40th Parallel, and the fruit of the bittersweet ripens orange.

When watermelons are ripe and firefly season comes to a close, then farmers and gardeners cut the last of the oats and put in fall peas.

When spiders start to increase their building of webs in the woodlot, then yellow jacket season begins in the windfall apples and plums, and morning fogs increase in the lowlands.

When the first field corn is mature, then gardeners divide and transplant the lily-of-the-valley.

When cardinals stop singing before dawn, the soybean leaves are yellowing in the fields and farmers start to cut corn for silage.

When velvetleaf goes to seed in Midwestern fields, then frost time approaches for pastures in the Rocky Mountains.

When long flocks of blackbirds move across the sky, then it's time for plums to be the sweetest of the year.

After last of the elderberries are picked, then second-brood corn borers, second-generation bean leaf beetles, and rootworm beetles work the fields.

When the first wild grape is sweet enough to eat, then farmers prepare the soil for the planting of winter grains.

When all the summer apples have been picked, then the first puffball mushroom of the year swells in cool, damp nights, and the wood thrush moves south across the Ohio River.

When there is more than one Judas maple tree in the

woodlot, then hickory nutting season gets underway.

When red leaves appear on the Virginia creeper in Kentucky, then snow threatens gardens in central Canada.

When the last of the garden phlox die back, then ragweed time winds down and the year's final tier of wildflowers is budding: beggarticks, bur marigolds, asters, zigzag goldenrod.

When dogbane pods turn reddish brown in the fields, then wood nettle has gone to seed under the high canopy.

When elm trees start to turn, then mallards are flying south. Whip-poor-wills, cedar waxwings and catbirds follow.

When greenbrier berries are black, then prickly mallow blooms along the fencerows and almost all the oats crop is cut.

When arrowhead blooms in the waterways, then pale Asian lady beetles have begun their late-summer migration.

The Natural Calendar

The first week of August brings White Snakeroot, Boneset, Clearweed and Jumpseed Seasons. Ragweed Season spreads along the 40th Parallel, and the pollen count begins its slow climb from an average of 30 grains per cubic meter at the end of July to about 300 by the end of August. Blackberry Season and Grape Season have moved up to the Midwest from Kentucky as Black Walnut Leafdrop Season gathers momentum all across the nation. Stonecrop Season starts in the gardens of the Middle Atlantic region as Meadowlark Migration Season and Ruby-Throated Hummingbird Flocking Season get underway throughout the country

Daybook

1982: Blackberries are ripe at South Glen. Clearweed is blooming in the woods. Common hops in flower in the north bushes. Great ragweed heading up. Horseweed identified, has probably been blooming a week or so.

1987: Sparrows chattering in the north bushes this morning, crows on the south end of the village, starlings in the west tree lot. No summer cardinal, no dove, no blue jay song.

1988: At 3:30 a.m., katydids suddenly went silent. They'd been singing since I woke up at 2:00. Crickets still loud.

1989: Japanese knotweed budding in the yard. To Wisconsin: Chicory opened in the sun at 6:45 a.m., at the beginning of my trip, closed 2:20 p.m., Central Daylight Time, near Rockford, Illinois. Patches of brown parsnips all along the highway. Mullein and milkweed still full bloom. Much teasel brown, complete. Queen Anne's lace everywhere, black eyed Susans, trumpet vine, too. Most crown vetch, so strong in June through mid July, gone now. Some late moth mullein. Tall ragweed in bloom near Indianapolis, ironweed flowering there, and sundrops, birdsfoot trefoil. Wild lettuce throughout. Near Wisconsin, a few June parsnips still in bloom, trefoil common here, white sweet clover, too.

1990: First blue dayflower opened today. Balloon flower still full.

1996: When I came back from Minnesota a week ago, the red phlox had just opened in Yellow Springs-- putting their flowering date around the 26th of July. Now the whites and reds are in full bloom. Day lilies continue to be open at different locations about town, and in the yard, too. Hosta leaves continue to disintegrate. It is the peak of all the coneflowers, and ironweed has finally budded. All the crops – from fruits to vegetables – in the whole country are weeks behind schedule because of the cool summer. My garden tomatoes are still not ripe. No cardinals heard in the morning. The chatter of sparrows, singsong of robins missing. One blue jay heard this morning at about 6:20. One yellow jacket seen, the first I've noticed.

1998: The first white and yellow arrowhead flowers are open in the pond, have been blooming no more than a day or two.

1999: First ironweed flowers seen this morning. Flax continues to bloom. Spiderwort has died back over the past two weeks, now completely gone. Heliopsis rusting, showy coneflowers peaking and turning toward autumn. Only a few fireflies at night; the drought never let them really come out. But this morning at 5:00, the Late Summer crickets were singing, along with a chorus of robins and cardinals. Cutting back the garden this afternoon, I flushed a giant Cecropia moth from its place in the weeds. It lumbered out into the sun, then settled into the weeds at the east end of the undergrowth.

2001: Last flowers on the last spike of the purple loosestrife. Several large cottonwoods completely yellow along the freeway.

2002: No birds at 4:25 a.m. Then cardinals were singing by 4:50. Jays joined at 5:00, then doves, then and crows within just a few more minutes.

2003: Burdock just opening in the South Glen. Scattered walnut leaves yellow and fallen, stuck to the touch-me-nots and wood nettle. Spider webs common across the paths. Resurrection lilies blooming along Dayton Street. Three tiger swallowtails and one monarch seen in the garden. Jeanie reports seeing several monarchs flying across the road this afternoon.

2006: Grackles call in the alley this morning at about 8:00 a.m. A couple of robins, five or six starlings seen there too, but only the grackles were vocal. Yesterday starlings noticed on the high wires, not a big flock, but maybe a couple of dozen. Another monarch and tiger swallowtail today. The hummingbird has finally found the feeder Jeanie put out earlier in July.

2007: Golden pollen fully emerged on the tall ragweed in the alley. Monarchs, tiger swallowtails, black swallowtails, fritillaries visit the garden. One giant swallowtail with its telltale yellow stripe came to the circle garden at noon. Robins and cardinals at about 5:00 this morning. A squirrel started whining about 7:00.

2008: Gillette, Wyoming to Cody, Wyoming through the Big Horn Mountains over Powder River Pass. The land became drier and more barren, and the wildflower growth thinned out. The yellow sweet clover gradually disappeared, as did the roadside sunflowers and the purple bush clover. In the mountains, some new bright blue flowers seen, a large, fat thistle-like plant, something like the massive, white Florida thistles.
 As we drove toward Buffalo, a pronghorn antelope ran in front

of the camper. Sagebrush and a yellow blooming tumble-weed-like plant increased as we approached Cody. In the central valley between Worlund and Cody, large fields of sugar beets. Intense heat for the past several days; today was probably close to 100 degrees. Now at 6:45, the RV is beginning to cool off a little.

2009: Cardinals at 4:53 a.m. They call for about an hour. Blue jays loud at 6:00. Anna Belle hydrangea flowers have lost most of their white. All around the yard, Asiatic dayflowers are opening.

2010: Cardinals at 4:55 a.m. Crows at 5:20. A very small robin found in the weed pile in the middle of the yard, its presence explaining yesterday's peeping all day by the mother robin. At 6:30 this evening, seven tiger swallowtails in the butterfly bush.

2011: Two more tiger swallowtails and several pearl crescents in the garden today. Cardinals for about an hour between five and six this morning, and a thunderous chorus of katydids and crickets as I sat outside between 7:45 and 8:30 p.m.

2012: Light robin and cardinal chorus at 5:00 this morning, crows calling, too. Tiger swallowtails and fritillaries at the butterfly bush off and on throughout the day. In the yard, Shasta daisies, Queen Anne's lace, and phlox are getting worn, most of the purple coneflowers gone, only a couple of buds remaining, zinnias, aging heliopsis and knockout roses, and showy coneflowers keeping up the garden color. Ironweed seen in bloom as we drove to Beavercreek (but only budding in the shade of the yard). At Bryan Park this evening, field thistles in flower, a large planting of what appears to be whorled coreopsis (where the cosmos field was last year) in late bloom, the last yellow petals on agrimony.

2013: A cardinal woke me up at 5:00. Crows strong at 6:00, becoming more active or vocal in town as autumn approaches. Four lilies still in bloom today. In the alley, euonymus vines are blooming. One giant swallowtail flew in front of me. Along Union Street, some taxus branches have three to four inches of new growth. All day, male tiger swallowtails were at the butterfly bushes, sometimes three at a time. One female tiger seen, one zebra swallowtail, and a fold-wing skipper. Steady clucking of starlings and grackles in the back trees throughout the afternoon. Resurrection lilies budded in front of Gerard's and along Limestone Street. Lil's burning bush has a red blush on its south leaves. This evening at Ellis Pond, field crickets all around us as we walked, loud chirping, whistling, buzzing crickets and katydids at 10:00 p.m. The weather was cool throughout the day, like it has been all week, an unusual spell that occurs (according to my records) only once in a decade.

2014: Last year's once-in-a-decade cool spell: it happened again this year. I walked into their back yard at 4:55 this morning – a cardinal sang far off; when I went out the front door at 5:00, I entered full robin and cardinal song. The cardinals sang and sang, the robins stopped in about ten minutes. Crows and a blue jay bell call at 5:23. In the background all the while, the static of ground crickets.
    Eleven lilies in bloom today. A Giant Swallowtail swooped down on the zinnias this morning, then was gone over the honeysuckles, and a monarch flew across the road in front of me as I was coming back from John Bryan Park.

2015: I got up early (the sky clear, full moon high in the southwest, air cool and dry), planned to listen to the very first cardinal of the day, but I misjudged the time, went out at 4:45, and the local cardinal was already in full song, an especially elaborate, uninhibited warbling. No morning robinsong since at least July 17th. Many small golden skippers playing in the sun today; I haven' seen them for a long time. Silver spotted skippers and male tiger swallowtails visited the zinnias and tithonia frequently through the day, and the second monarch of the summer floated by.

2016: A male tiger swallowtail noticed in the circle garden zinnias, as I was getting ready to go to the shop. Now it seems that the number of butterflies is increasing for the first time this summer. Another tiger in the afternoon zinnias.

2017: Elderberries completely ripe along Elm Street.

2018: A cool and cloudy day. One tattered Eastern black swallowtail followed me around the yard. Three lilies, among them Jeanie's Stargazer, and the buds of the sedum I transplanted near the porch last fall are showing pink. Late in the afternoon, I looked outside, saw a monarch and a male tiger swallowtail. The katydids began to sing at 8:16 this evening, two minutes later than yesterday evening. Then as I sat listening, an adolescent skunk walked by my feet and disappeared into the potting area of the porch.

  At the Covered Bridge habitat: pale violet bee balm, early ironweed, some wingstem (seemed past its prime), tall nettle and wood nettle blooming and vigorous, late burdock, woodland sunflower, black-eyed Susan, germander, tall bell flower, late swamp milkweed, gray-headed coneflower, tall coneflower,

One becomes then a geographer of the micro-region, if not always a very good one, putting together, perhaps not wittingly, a mental composite of features that tell of home: a profile of hillside, the hue and texture of houses, the pitch of church steeples, the color of cattle.

  David E. Sopher, "The Landscape of Home"

August 2nd
The 214th Day of the Year

*I will love you in the thyme-leafed speedwell,
I will love you by the Ragweed Moon.*

Hepatica Sun

Sunrise/set: 5:34/7:48
Day's Length: 14 hours 14 minutes
Average High/Low: 85/64
Average Temperature: 75
Record High: 98 – 1899
Record Low: 49 – 1965

Weather

Cool morning temperatures in the 50s occur today 25 percent of all the years, but afternoons in the 90s come 30 percent of the time, 80s sixty percent, and 70s just ten percent. The Sun shines at least a little on nine out of ten August 2nds, but thundershowers pass through 35 percent of the time.

Natural Calendar

As Middle Summer comes to a close, ragweed pollen fills the humid afternoons, wood nettle goes to seed in the bottomlands, honeysuckle berries and wild cherries ripen, and hickory nuts and black walnuts drop into the undergrowth.

Blackberries are ready to eat when ragweed blossoms. And the season's second-last wave of wildflowers – the Joe Pye weed, monkey flower, tall coneflower, clearweed, horseweed, white snakeroot, jumpseed, prickly mallow, virgin's bower, false boneset, field thistle and Japanese knotweed – bloom in the open fields and along the fence rows.

Golden and purple coneflowers, and red, pink and violet phlox still rule the gardens. Orange-and-gold-flowered trumpet vines still curl through trellises. Ephemeral resurrection lilies briefly replace the day lilies, the Asiatic lilies and the Oriental lilies. Mums and stonecrop start to color the dooryards.

In the shade of the woods, leafcup is the dominant flower, touch-me-nots beginning to complement its bloom. Along the lakeshores, arrowhead flowers as rusty dodder winds through the tattered black raspberry bushes.

The Stars

August is the month of the Milky Way in the eastern early night sky. Cygnus the Swan can be found there, its formation a giant cross or like a goose in flight. Below it is Aquila, spreading from its keystone, Altair, like a great eagle. Almost directly overhead, Vega, of the constellation Lyra, is the brightest star in the heavens. Hercules stands beside it. June's Corona Borealis and the huge Arcturus have moved to the west. An hour or two before sunrise, Orion rises, in the same position it holds after dark on Christmas Eve. The Pleiades and Taurus are almost overhead. Cygnus sets in the northwest.

Daybook

1984: White cabbage butterflies are spiraling, mating near the barn-board fence. One female rested on a leaf of honeysuckle, and the male returned to her over and over, so light, in ethereal, erotic randori, in perfect balance with the air and with the other.

1987: South Glen: Swallowtails and monarchs all along the path, a great blue heron upstream. I had a brief encounter with a weasel, its coat so rich and blue-brown, almost ironweed-purple in the sun. Hickory nuts on the ground, acorns near full size. Plenty of wild blackberries for breakfast as I walked. Wild cherries half turned.

1989: Madison, Wisconsin: White snakeroot starting to bloom, like in Yellow Springs, but water cress, still flowering like late June in Ohio. Milkweed pods well formed, spurge full bloom, burdock full with some burs, a few white vervain, most white snakeroot budding with a few in bloom. Early bull thistles. Avens to burs, enchanter's nightshade with burs, agrimony late. Goldenrod in early bloom. Green berries on the elderberry. Deptford pink, gray headed coneflower, wild quinine, hoary vervain, monarda, cup plant (*Silphium perfoliatum*), gay feather, wild lettuce, white sweet clover, naked sunflower *(Helianthus occidentalis)*, early ironweed, compass plant, rattlesnake master, bristly thistle, tall cinquefoil. Ragweed, eight feet tall, in bloom: its calendar is the same throughout the thousands of miles of my trips.

1992: Two goldfinches in the zinnias and cosmos today, yellow in the reds and purples.

1993: Late evening: A lone goose flies honking over the park, the first goose of Late Summer.

1996: The first katydid sang tonight in the yard. Resurrection lilies are in full bloom at scattered locations in town; ours are emerging but not flowering.

1998: Ironweed full early bloom along the freeway. Only one water lily open in the pond.

1999: At six this morning, total silence, no birds at all. Three water lilies opened today. But no resurrection lilies yet.

2000: Tonight at 8:00, no birds heading to their roosts, no swallows, no bats. Full cicada song. One bat and then the full katydids and crickets at 8:08, then the cicadas fade into the dark. An odd sharp whinny in the back trees at 8:10 like a cross between a squirrel and an owl and a pileated woodpecker; repeated maybe ten times, then silence.

2001: As I did tai chi this morning, a locust leaf fluttered to the ground. Later, I looked out the window: another leaf was coming down.

2002: Into South Glen: Spitbugs still hanging on the grasses. Tall bellflowers still open, the last teasel, wood nettles and avens blooming, ironweed coming in, a few blackberries ripe – but small and bitter from the June and July drought. Spider webs across the paths. Buckeye leaves rusting and falling beside the black walnuts. Some hickory nuts down. The locust trees along Corey Street are brown from leafminers. Resurrection lilies full bloom in town, two budded in the south garden. First yellow jacket seen. Fireflies at

7:40 p.m.

2003: Three monarchs in the north garden all at once this morning. Tiger swallowtails appear consistently at the butterfly bush. Another monarch in the afternoon in the south garden.

2005: Another wave of 90-degree temperatures settles in; plants begin to droop by late morning. A total of only about two dozen lily blossoms remain on about a dozen plants. Albert, the green frog, still croaks from time to time – once this morning early, again at noon. Cicadas loud and strong from sunup until dark.

2006: Cardinals sang at 4:51 a.m. Doves joined in about half an hour later, continued off and on through the early morning. One male tiger swallowtail lazily sipped impatiens and rose of Sharon at 8:00. Pairs of orange fold-wing skippers were playing in tight randori in the morning sun. A cardinal suddenly came out from the bushes, hovered for an instant and then gobbled one of the skippers down. In the alley, giant ragweed is getting pollen and the first burdock blooms have appeared. Wild blue chicory is lush, complementing the purple garden phlox in Mrs. Timberlake's yard. In our yard, new black-eyed Susans create the dominant color. Leaves trickle to the undergrowth, one every few minutes.

2007: First ironweed flowers in the yard.

2008: Cody, Wyoming to Yellowstone National Park: Jeanie and I saw hundreds of buffalo, a giant elk, a flock of white pelicans and a flock of black-headed ducks as we drove around the lower loop of the park. A wide variety of wildflowers are in bloom between Cody and Yellowstone including Evert's thistle (elk thistle), common timothy, silvery lupine, heal all, roundleaf harebell, the pale violet Pacific aster (*Aster chilensis*), common cow parsnip, a few red castilleja (paintbrush), pussy toes, sulfur buckwheat, short Missouri goldenrod, common yarrow, common yampah, possible tall *Tofieldia,* possible crested wheatgrass, large-petaled water lilies, and others photographed.

2009: The red monarda and almost all the lilies are gone. The violet monarda holds at maybe a third of its color, complementing the full Joe Pye weed and the remaining pink mallow. Near the porch, the giant red hibiscus plants have four flowers. In the northeast garden, the purple coneflowers and Queen Anne's lace are dominant. Violet hosta flowers offer some color along the north side of the house. Tat in Madison says all of her lilies ended last week. Katydids calling after dark. In the dooryard garden, the budded stonecrop promises a bright late August and early September.

2010: Robins and cardinals strong from about 5:00 to 5:20 this morning. As I was talking to Tat on the phone this morning, I counted eight male tiger swallowtails on the butterfly bush – the most so far this year – and the most ever for me. Only two fireflies seen in the backyard in the span of half an hour tonight.

2011: Record heat continues. Two tiger swallowtails, two Eastern commas, two crescents, many silver-spotted skippers and cabbage whites. Intense song from tree crickets, field crickets and katydids at dusk.

2012: Doves, robins and cardinals and loud tree crickets when I went outside at 5:15 this morning, and continuing off and on throughout the morning. Crab apple foliage turning in the park, some trees losing leaves. Cicadas dying along the sidewalk, but cicada calls still strong throughout the day. White bindweed blooming in the yard. Peaches full size and blushing. The wind light and hot. Robin vespers this evening.

2013: More mild weather, fog at dawn. Six lilies hold in the garden, eight scattered blossoms. Gladioli continue to come in slowly, their season in town having opened around July 25th. Violet monarda almost gone beneath the full Joe Pye. Male tiger swallowtails continuing to visit the butterfly bushes and the zinnias. The neighborhood deer ate off all the peach-colored gladiolus flowers some time this afternoon.

2014: Eleven lilies in bloom today, numbers holding, thanks to a couple of rebloomers. One skipper seen in the garden, and at Ellis

Pond a brown, blending perfectly with the bark of a Siberian elm.

2015: Nine lily plants in bloom, and only rebloomers have more than one blossom. Butterflies continue to visit the garden: Eastern blacks, skippers, whites, male tigers, a giant swallowtail.

2016: Just a little time at home today: two lily blossoms, one male tiger swallowtail. The prairie dock is budded at the corner of High and West South College Streets.

2017: Resurrection lilies still hold along Dayton Street and in the yard. One monarch sped through the garden in the morning, too fast for me to make a positive identification. Then in the late afternoon when I was getting ready to walk downtown, a zebra swallowtail showed up at the zinnias in the circle garden.

2018: Heavy fog throughout the area this morning, and light overcast throughout the day. Butterflies in the garden: a monarch and two male tiger swallowtail. A brief cardinal vespers at 7:35 this evening. The katydids began to sing at 8:09, three minutes earlier than yesterday evening. And a few minutes later, yesterday's skunk came walking by me.

The invisible shapes of smells, rhythms of cricketsong, and of movement of shadows all, in a sense, provide the subtle body of our thoughts.

David Abram

August 3rd
The 215th Day of the Year

The backyard
overgrown with wild grape,
hollyhock, creeping Charlie,
is home to a thousand
white butterflies this August....

Ann Filemyr

Sunrise/set: 5:35/7:47
Day's Length: 14 hours 12 minutes
Average High/Low: 85/64
Average Temperature: 75
Record High: 100 – 1964
Record Low: 40 – 1965

Weather
Highs in the 90s come 40 percent of the time on this date, 80s fifty percent, with 70s ten percent. Skies are clear to partly cloudy eight years in a decade, with rain passing through one year in three. Most night lows are in the 60s, just 20 percent reaching into the 50s.

Natural Calendar
Across the Midwest, almost all of the corn is silking by now, and a third of the crop could be in dough. Two-thirds of the soybeans are flowering or setting pods. Oats and the second cut of alfalfa, running neck and neck, are ordinarily three-fourths harvested. Farmers are making corrective lime and fertilizer applications for August and September seeding.

Daybook
1984: To the Swinging Bridge in the North Glen: First boneset and white snakeroot seen blooming. Hobblebush done flowering, most mint complete. More red Virginia creeper leaves falling to the grass. Damselflies and spitbugs continue their activity. An ambush

bug and a new flower, water hemlock, discovered. Some touch-me-not-pods are bursting. White vervain, tall bellflower and lopseed holding on. Sweet clover has gone to brittle seeds.

1985: South Glen: Osage fruit seems full size now, the first fallen to the path. Small-flowered agrimony identified, and showy coneflower, and a very rare biennial gaura. Wild cucumbers throughout. Hickory nuts common on the ground.

1988: Now two weeks after the rains, the tall coneflowers have started to come in. Joe Pye weed and monkey flower are in full bloom near the Swinging Bridge. Lizard's tail has turned into long, white seed heads. First oxeyes bloom, along with the ragweed. Large green seeds noticed on the waterleaf, *Hydrophyllum canadense*. Purslane and speedwell now cover the garden. Great blue heron seen on the way home.

1989: To northern Minnesota: Spotted knapweed found north of Madison, Wisconsin, same stage as in the mountains of eastern Pennsylvania thirty days before; Canadian thistle – which had gone to seed six weeks ago in Yellow Springs – was in full bloom near Eau Claire. Day lilies still fresh, and June's yellow and white sweet clover were still open in Minneapolis; and the plantings of crown vetch along the freeways were strong (gone in Yellow Springs). Some winter wheat was still in the fields. Some fields of oats were still being harvested. Northern goldenrod, ahead of the southern variety of Greene County, was in full bloom. And milkweed pods were half formed, just like in Glen Helen. Many other common flowers from Ohio north of the Twin Cities: sow thistles, St. John's wort, chicory, sundrops, great mullein, Joe Pye weed, bouncing bets, black-eyed Susans, Queen Anne's lace, bird's foot trefoil, parsnips, horseweed, common and great ragweed.

1992: A couple of weeks ago, I found a bumblebee motionless on its side in the middle of a red zinnia: yellow and black, soft, at rest in the flower at its peak. I wondered if he had been poisoned along his pollen rounds. I shook the flower lightly, but the bee didn't move. I left him for dead; but the next morning he was gone.

Today I found another silent bumblebee in another red zinnia. This time, I was more persistent; and when I stroked his wings, he recovered, got up clumsily and buzzed away. He and the other, I presume, had only been sleeping in the sun, exhausted, or drugged with nectar, collapsed in this bright, benign bed, indifferent to enemies and duty.

1993: A cool evening, fireflies blinking in the grass, not one flying.

1996: Fireflies nearly gone. First blue Asiatic dayflower blooms along the north wall. Day lilies almost gone about town. Cabbage butterflies in groups of three or four today. Yellow swallowtail, blue swallowtail seen.

1997: Return from a trip to Canton about 175 miles northeast of Yellow Springs to see Jeni: First goldenrod opening near Bolivar. Very early sundrops, a few purple ironweeds, a few wingstems. Joe Pye weed common, waves of blue chicory and Queen Anne's lace. A few blue dayflowers seen. People at the bed and breakfast said they had been out picking blackberries. Locusts along the highway browning from leaf miners. Yellow patches in the scrub cottonwoods.

1999: Full robin valediction song in the front yard at nine this morning, loud singsong. Unlike the gentle, monotonous mating and nesting melodies, this was more earnest and more eloquent. And it lasted for minutes, seeming to be a prolonged, melodic cry, a wild lament for the end of summer. This afternoon, Louis the cat caught a snake that was in the process of eating an angleworm.

2000: The mallow holds surprisingly well at late bloom. A few red bergamot have blossomed out of time, the pond arrowhead is now in full bloom (after its first blossoms in July died back). One last Oriental lily holds in the north garden, the orange tiger Turk's cap. And the small *Stella d'oro* lilies still bloom at the malls and along the south wall. August hostas, Sum and Substance, Royal Standard, starting to flower. The August Moon hostas are almost done. Fallen apples bothersome in the yard now. I keep stumbling over them. No frogs calling in the pond this year. But Suzy complains about the crows, so loud.

2001: Deep sense of Late Summer now at South Glen: patches of red Virginia creeper, some buckeye trees almost completely bare, some wood nettle leaves turning white. Joe Pye weed going to seed. Apples are lying all about the yard. Resurrection lilies still at full bloom throughout town.

2002: Yellow jacket seen eating a ladybug.

2005: Cricket hunters now.

2006: Snout-nosed butterflies swarming into southern Texas by the billions. The news says that "conditions are ideal" in Mexico for their breeding. This is a high period for all types of butterflies in that region. Here at home, more monarchs and swallowtails seen in the yard. Skippers continue to play throughout the mornings. Resurrection lilies noticed in full bloom along Don's fence. Coming back from Beavercreek, Jeanie and I saw a large flock of starlings feeding in a suburban lawn. The first major flocking of Late Summer?

2007: A pair of catbirds has moved into the yard this week, flying back and forth with nesting materials. Their meow-like call heard for the first time during breakfast. In the alley, euonymus is in full bloom, as are tall coneflowers and thin-leafed/small-flowered coneflowers. The first pokeweed berries noticed turning purple. Mateo's black walnut tree is starting to turn, and other black walnuts along Limestone Street are losing their summer green, becoming dusky. Along the front sidewalk, jumpseed plants are open all the way. At home, four winter tomato seeds (Cobra variety) I planted for December have sprouted. Lilies are down to half a dozen plants with one bloom each, but the lush rose of Sharon, the large-flowered hibiscus and the second bloom of roses fill giant holes in the waning summer. Monarchs and swallowtails continue to visit.

2008: Yellowstone National Park: Returned to the Gibbon River and then drove north on the high, winding road toward the grand vistas near the northeast entrance. Saw blue star grass, wild geranium (*Viscosissimum*), fireweed, a magenta fringed gentian-like plant, something like the "monument plant" or *Frasera speciosa*, a tall, green mullein-like plant, a few *Rubus idaeus*, native red raspberry with tiny fruit just set, *Phlox multiflora* – a small, white ground cover phlox near the campsite, and *Helianthella uniflora* or showy goldeneye or *H. quinqueneruis* as the common roadside sunflower like plant.

2009: Cool morning, almost crisp, a feel of September in the air. In the new cherry tree, a mother sparrow was feeding two babies.

2010: North down the alley, I found a red mulberry trees still full of dark mulberries. Fewer tiger swallowtails came to the butterfly bushes today, only three seen at one time through the afternoon.

2011: Heat continues, cicadas, crickets, katydids fill the days and evenings. Two sparrow fledglings still being fed by their parents. Purple coneflowers are way past their best. Phlox, Joe Pye, a few last orange lilies, Endless Summer hydrangeas, late hostas, gooseneck, heliopsis, zinnias, rudbeckia, and dahlias hold color in the garden. On my walk after supper with Bella, I found an Osage fruit full size by the side of the road.

2012: At 5:00, strong robin singsong, distant cardinals, doves nearby, tree crickets dominant. Few butterflies today, one hummingbird moth, a few cabbage butterflies, one spicebush. Euonymus seen in full bloom along High Street. Robin vespers when I was out at 6:50. Light cooling breeze.

2013: Only four lily blossoms today. Male tiger swallowtails in the garden off and on throughout the day.

2014: Seven lily plants in bloom today – although the number of blossoms is more like a dozen. For the first time this summer, a long-bodied spider (long-jawed orb-weaver) has made an elaborate web above the pond. Into South Glen for just a little while: Rich, soft mounds of yellow touch-me-nots and what seems like acres of wood nettle, tall imposing, its flowers spread like miniature ferns. A patch of tall bell flowers, maybe half a dozen, the first real grouping I've seen of them here. Leafcup common. Beggarticks grown lush, waist high, wingstem open.

2015: Seven lilies in bloom. Sparrow feeding its fledgling on the feeder. Strong cardinal vespers at dusk.

2016: The giant red hibiscus near the north end of the porch blossomed over night. North east to Keuka Lake in upper New York state, an uneventful trip (white snakeroot, Queen Anne's Lace) except for the first goldenrod seen in bloom east of Chautauqua. Fringed loosestrife and boneset flowering along the backroads by the lake.

2017: Walking home from downtown as a storm approached, wind pulling down yellow black walnut leaves.

2018: Two monarchs, one Eastern black, one male tiger swallowtail, several white-spotted skippers, cabbage whites in the zinnias this morning, sky cloudless, dew on the grass. The Stargazer lily continues in bloom, and the first flower of the Royal Standard hosta opened in the night, the same time as in 2000. First gray on the Joe Pye flowers. In the afternoon, a great spangled fritillary, a hackberry butterfly, a male tiger swallowtail, a monarch, several silver-spotted skippers and cabbage whites, this evening a giant swallowtail, the last butterfly of the day.

The almanac of time hangs in the brain:
The seasons numbered, by the inward sun....

Dylan Thomas

August 4th
The 216th Day of the Year

And so zeitgebers such as lilies or parsnips followed north across the landscape become wells from which time emerges and retreats. Like metaphors, the flowers take the place of what they signify, become fountainheads of stability, offer immanence that persists within renewal and history.

Paul Quel

Sunrise/set: 5:36/7:46
Day's Length: 14 hours 10 minutes
Average High/Low: 85/64
Average Temperature: 74
Record High: 99 – 1887
Record Low: 48 – 1912

Weather

Continued hot and very humid most years. Highs reach the 90s forty-percent of the time; there is a 45 percent chance of 80s, only 15 percent for 70s. Thanks to the arrival of the August 4th cool front, the likelihood of rain increases to 60 percent, the highest since July 3, and the second highest of the summer. Clouds block the sun all day three years in a decade. There is just a ten percent chance of a cool low below 60.

Natural Calendar

In the mornings, cardinals and doves still sing, starting half an hour before dawn, often continuing through the day, often greeting the night with vespers. Blue jays still care for their young, whining and flitting through the bushes, but starlings and warblers become more restless. In some years, the robins give long singsong performances. Cicadas compete with the crickets at dusk.

Daybook

1983: To Grinnell Swamp: Great and common ragweed in bloom, avens with green burs, wood mint still in bloom, a few white snakeroot plants open, agrimony, leafcup, tall bell flower, daisy fleabane, germander, tall coneflower, wood nettle, moth mullein, sundrops in flower. First jumpseed blossoms found. May apples still hold their fruit.

1984: At South Glen, the sound of bees, a steady drone throughout my walk. First clearweed flower found, my first. Goldenrod budding. Most ironweed still not open. A few wingstem blooming. All milkweed is done, only couple milkweed beetles noticed. Blackberries ripe, and wild grapes are purple. A few box elder trees are yellowing at the tips. Wood nettle and oxeye are still in full flower. Some St. John's wort left, one loosestrife. Geese flew over 6:30 p.m.

1986: Cardinals still sing in the early morning. Fireflies gone. No geese flying over yet.

1988: A cardinal woke me up at 4:55 a.m.

1989: Northern Minnesota, John's farm outside of New York Mills: Wheat being harvested. Ragweed in bloom, and amaranth, black medic, bristly thistle, thimble plant, clot bur (*Xanthium strumarium*), yarrow, goosefoot, catmint, wild sage, white campion, burdock, goldenrod, sow thistle, meadow goat's beard, birdsfoot trefoil, purple vetch, Canadian thistle. Milkweed pods half formed. John says frost comes quickly at the end of August. Foliage is gone from the trees by the end of September. Spring comes suddenly toward the end of April, engulfs May.

1992: At Caesar Creek on a small stump protruding from the lake: monkey flower, cinquefoil, water horehound in full bloom. Plants on another stump included ragweed and small-flowered asters. Along the shore, tall coneflowers, oxeyes and Queen Anne's lace. At my fishing hole, the dodder was orange like it was last year, but the tree line was deep green, no sign of fall. This evening at home, geese flew over honking at 5:30 p.m.

1993: A little after sunrise: light rain, gray, hardly any birds at the feeders, no cardinals singing, no sparrows, no dove calls, no blue jays. Grackles gone from the back trees. When the sun came out a few hours later, the birds were back and noisy. Three yellow swallowtails in the yard today. Scent of Late Summer deepening, late haying, moist decay, pollen, apples.

1996: A cardinal sang off and on this morning, beginning near 5:30.

1999: Robin singsong, long and loud this morning like yesterday. At 8:00 a.m., the dogs across Dayton Street were barking and barking, and then the bullfrog joined in from the pond.

2001: First cardinal at 5:55 this morning, then more cardinals gradually joining in throughout the neighborhood for an hour or so. The full moon was golden, setting over Dayton, Venus and Jupiter close together in the east over Glen Helen. Blue jay bell call at 6:13, doves at 6:17, cardinals starting to feed in the old apple tree at 6:21. Jupiter disappeared into the sunlight by 6:30. Venus was finally gone at 6:45.

2002: Doves still calling in the mornings.

2004: Whistling crickets, probably tree crickets, heard this morning at 5:00.

2005: Short walk along the Orton Trail with Jeanie this morning, almost nothing in bloom except one small-flowered St. John's wort, the first white snakeroot, and a few late avens and leafcups. Ripe blackberries found, small and tart.

2006: Three tiger swallowtails in the Joe Pye weed this morning. Euonymus vines in the alley have green buds (they seem like fruit/berries, but they're buds) and a few of the first green flowers. The lilies are down to six blooming plants, and just around a dozen total blossoms.

2007: Sparrow seen feeding a fledging. The younger bird was much larger than the adult, maybe a cowbird dropped into the nest by its parent. A few purple berries on the panicled dogwood in the alley. Honeysuckle berries getting fatter in the yard.

2008: West from Yellowstone to Missoula, Montana: Butter and eggs (*Lunaria vulgaris*) along the roadside out of the park, very common. Reappearance of yellow sweet clover, a few milkweed, fields of knapweed. Haying between Butte and Missoula. Wide, wide vistas of mountains and big sky.

2010: Cardinals at 5:00 and singing for about half an hour, baby sparrows still being fed. One monarch and two tiger swallowtails, one spicebush swallowtail at the butterfly bush today. A few yellow black walnut leaves drifted down to High Street when I passed by with Bella. A giant green caterpillar of the polyphemus moth has eaten almost an entire potted tomato plant.

2011: Cardinal song for an hour, starting at 4:45 a.m. Three monarchs, three yellow tiger swallowtails, one spicebush swallowtail, one crescent seen today. In an early evening walk, steady call of like-tree crickets, chirps from field crickets when I passed by, cicadas strong.

2012: Robin chorus when I got up at 4:15. Cardinals and crows heard from inside at 4:30. Romuald the frog croaking before the rain. Robins continuing to call through midmorning. The August 4th cool front is sweeping across the Midwest, clouds throughout most of the day.

2013: Again, cardinals around 5:00 woke me up. Four daylilies struggle to put out a blossom or two. Five yellow swallowtails counted at the butterfly bushes this afternoon. Resurrection lilies are open along Dayton Street, most likely their first or second day. At John Bryan Park, heal-all was the only fresh flower that I found in bloom, and only fragments of agrimony and white vervain were left. White snakeroot was budded. Driving by the Covered Bridge, I saw the first wingstem flowering, flanked by purple ironweed.

2014: Eight lily plants in bloom today. At Ellis Pond, I saw a male tiger swallowtail and a small black swallowtail.

2015: A sunny morning of seven lilies, one monarch, numerous gold skippers in randori, and one butterfly – maybe a brown or a Viceroy (it was loopy like a Viceroy) - driving a sparrow away from its perch – or following it in a case of mistaken identity. Cardinals singing and singing, maybe teaching their young (as do the robins with their guiding calls in Middle Summer). Looking back at the pattern of 2012, I find it curious how different the robinsong pattern was that year, how much later it went in the summer – a full month later, disappearing only on August 21. So the very early spring must have provided enough room for an extra brood or at least an extra month of frolicking. This evening along the bike path: touch-me-nots gathering momentum, one Virginia creeper with veins and shades of rust and red, cardinal vespers.

2016: First jumpseed flowers opened at Moya's.

2017: The August 4 cool front arrived on schedule with a thunderstorm and a low in the lower 50s. In Portland, Oregon, heat in the 90s and 100s continues. Cardinal woke me up at 5:00 a.m. Jill's vervain has headed up.

2018: One lily: Jeanie's stargazer holds. Tat reports her Joe Pye weed very much to seed now, even ahead of mine. One monarch quiet in a red zinnia this cool morning. A spicebush butterfly in front of the post office, flying back and forth as though waiting for someone. A male tiger swallowtail and a zebra swallowtail seen when I went outside at noon. A second day of clearing out in the north gardens: trying to manicure a little and to open up space for the zinnias to show, tying back the fallen tithonias. The large south hackberry tree has been shedding for several days, small slivers of leaves. This evening, 7:15, sweet, long cardinal vespers, and again at 7:35 and again at 7:45. A new cricket call tonight, loud, intermittent, maybe three or four seconds long. Katydids at 8:05, three minutes earlier than three days ago.

The universe is a communion of subjects, not a collection of objects.
Thomas Berry

August 5th
The 217th Day of the Year

It is the August also of my life,
And I, too, stand for a moment on a height,
Like an elm tree musing, a dark arrested fountain,
Over a far prospect, where a river swings in silent, silver arcs,
And those two restless hounds, mind and heart,
Lie quiet at my feet.

Clara Shanafelt

Sunrise/set: 5:37/7:45
Day's Length: 14 hours 8 minutes
Average High/Low: 85/64
Average Temperature: 74
Record High: 103 – 1918
Record Low: 45 – 1972

Weather

Today's highs are shared equally between the 80s and 90s, thirty-five percent chances of each, with a 30 percent possibility for an afternoon in the 70s. Rain falls four years out of ten. Totally cloudy skies are likely one year in four. Cool nights in the 50s occur about 30 percent of the time. The sharp contrast with yesterday's averages shows the effect of the August 4th high-pressure system.

Natural Calendar

Butterflies often become more common this week of the year, monarchs appearing more frequently, and another generation of cabbage butterflies, swallowtails and skippers seeking nectar. Sometimes giant imperial moths come out to seek the lights of the city. Tiny alypias, shiny black moths with white spots on their wings, may find their way indoors.

Daybook

1982: Queen Anne's lace and chicory still dominate the roadsides, with tall thistles, horseweed, wild lettuce, milkweed (most with pods now), teasel and mullein (both turning brown). Wingstem becoming prominent. Ragweed early full bloom. Crickets and katydids fill the night.

1983: Mullein and teasel are still in full bloom. Daylilies are gone, but trumpet creepers are still blooming, Joe Pye Weed is strong, and ironweed is just opening. Oxeyes and black-eyed Susans and other sunflowers and wingstem are also prominent. No trees turning except the honey locusts near Wilberforce. Common hops flowering on the back hedge.

1984: First blue dayflower opens in the yard.

1985: A cool, cloudy day, high only in the low 70s, the first pivot toward fall this year.

1986: Jacoby: No fish biting. The river is quiet, dry leaves drifting to the water. Finches and swallowtails all around me. Ragweed just getting pollen. Some wild cherries black. On the way back to the car, I came across a black walnut on the path; one seen on the ground in town just a couple days ago. Fall moving down one nut at a time.

1988: Puffball mushroom, 72 inches in diameter, reported found in the woods near Dayton, after a week of days in the 90s, humid. Puffball season: it's almost fall.

1990: South to Georgia: Trees yellowing from Yellow Springs to the Gulf coast: sycamores, poplars, sweet gum, birch, cottonwood, linden, red bud. Locust leaves laced from skeletonizers. Scattered goldenrod throughout. Wild lettuce and horseweed dying at Jekyll Island, strong throughout most of the East.

1991: To Caesar Creek: The drought seems to have turned the leaves early. Sycamore, dogwood, poplar, cottonwood, buckeye show Early Fall tans and rusts that mix with Late Summer's wildflower purple and gold. Long patches of red poison ivy and Virginia creeper near the dark water. Dodder in and across the wild raspberries, turning orange. Box elders and elms are paling. One catfish, nice size, at the new hole, 3:03 p.m. Cicadas loud. But they keep to their trees. The annual cicadas rarely get lost on the water. The red, periodic ones, are the passionate, reckless fliers. Yellow bullhead at 3:27. Few birds today, except for a catbird across the channel, a crow and a heron off in the distance. No blackbirds, flickers, or red-headed woodpeckers. Fewer insects. Carp wallowing in the shallows to my right, slurping as though it were still June. My line has bites every 20 minutes or so as though the fish were going back and forth across the area, sweeping it for food.

1992: Stonecrop starts to bloom.

1997: Another monarch butterfly in the yard.

1998: No water lilies on the pond this morning, the first time since they started in the spring. At the far end of High Street, the giant prairie dock has opened. Along the freeway, white teasel has replaced the violet teasel. In Cincinnati, Japanese anemone opens with its purple flower. Oak-leaf viburnum flowers have darkened. Now is the time for white-petaled viburnum. Full coneflower season continues. Red jumpseed found at the zoo. Cottonwoods in retreat, yellowing quickly.

1999: Crows, doves, cardinals at about 5:00 this morning. The frog still calls from the pond. Robin sing-songing by 6:00.

2000: North Glen with Mike: Great blue lobelia, jumpseed, yellow touch-me-nots (without any seed pods to pop), small-flowered agrimony, a few avens, white vervain, some early low goldenrod beginning, one enchanter's nightshade. Indigo bunting seen, red-eyed vireo and a blue-billed cuckoo.

2001: I'm hearing crows again in the morning. Is that because I'm listening for them, or are they really starting to become active again, reforming into bands for the fall and winter?

2002: At 4:30 a.m., silence, then distant cardinals. At 5:00, prominent cardinals, doves, even a robin song. At 5:10, crows join in. By 5:30, the cicadas have started, and the birdsong diminishes.

2003: This evening, crickets and katydids were loud and strong for the first time all year.

2004: After the one monarch butterfly in late July, only swallowtails, two or three a day, noticed in the garden.

2005: Yellow walnut leaves fall on Dayton Street, yellow mulberry leaves into the back yard. Resurrection lilies full on Winter Street. Five different lily plants in bloom. Royal Standard hosta budding. Gladiolas full in the village. Second blossom of the pink spirea holds. Yellow tiger swallowtail and spicebush swallowtail in aerial randori this afternoon. Greg called this evening: he found baby skunks that were four-inches long.

2006: Rich blue chicory continues to bloom in Mateo's lawn. Resurrection lilies found in bloom by the Korean lilac bush – I'd forgotten about planting them there. Golden fold-wing skippers keep up their morning play, glittering in the sunlight. s and tiger swallowtails continue to visit the zinnias and Joe Pye.

2008: From Missoula, Montana to Pasco, Washington, about five hours or so from Portland: The first half of the drive produced a variety of old and new plants: white and yellow sweet clover, white campion, short goldenrod, wild lettuce, knapweed, then miles of great mullein still in bloom, scattered moth mullein, St. John's wort, a tall yellow trefoil, a tansy-looking plant widespread, and a likely tall goldenrod. The morning was bright and cool as we drove across western Montana. We had lunch at the lake at Coeur d'Alene, the water clear as it was 50 years ago, Jeanie said. Then into eastern Washington, barren and brown and hot. All across the hills, however, the wheat harvest was underway.

2010: Only a few cardinal calls, one robin song around 5:00 this morning, then quiet. The polyphemus caterpillar had disappeared during the night. A soft rain at seven. Blue jay whining and robin burbling throughout the morning. Two yellow tiger swallowtails and one monarch seen today.

2011: A giant swallowtail and a tiger this morning before we left for Oregon. Yesterday afternoon, Catherine called, excited to say she had seen her first giant swallowtail.

2012: Robins and cardinals still sing before dawn.

2013: Into South Glen: Full bloom of yellow touch-me-nots at the entrance along the highway. Late wood nettle blossoms, a few tall bellflowers, leafcup, Queen Anne's lace common in bloom. Fresh heal-all flowering, very early wingstem and ironweed. A polygonia butterfly, a crescent spot butterfly, a woodland sunflower, a Deptford pink, a late fleabane seen. White snakeroot budding, black walnut trees turning a little throughout the woods, many walnut leaves on the path. Woodmint graying, shaggy. Blackberries ripe, sweet.

2014: Seven lilies (including the first naked lady/resurrection lily) blooming today, only one plant with multiple blossoms. The first two large red hibiscus flowers opened over night. (The first of the pink ones opened on the 26th.) A male tiger swallowtail spent a long time in the zinnias at midday. Alice reported seeing at least a dozen monarchs when she visited Michigan.

2015: Clear and cool at dawn: cardinals, jays, red-bellied woodpeckers, nuthatches, chickadees, crows, and a couple of robin calls, one robin in the street. The village gardens: thin-leafed (small-flowered) coneflowers, purple phlox, purple coneflowers, showy golden coneflowers, gray-headed coneflowers, Shasta daisies, bright red hibiscus.

2018: Hot and clear, cicadas loud, sparrows feeding and chirping, the house wren scolding. A monarch around 9:00 a.m. and swallowtails off and on through the day. The katydids began to call at 8:01 this evening..

*The flat fruit of the locust fell, lying like curved blades in the grass.
August ripened the sedge clumps.*

James Still

August 6th
The 218th Day of the Year

No marigolds yet closed are;
No shadows great appear;
Nor doth the early shepherd's star
Shine like a spangle here.

Robert Herrick

Sunrise/set: 5:38/7:43
Day's Length: 14 hours 5 minutes
Average High/Low: 85/64
Average Temperature: 74
Record High: 101 – 1918
Record Low: 49 – 1994

Weather

Thirty percent chance of a high in the 90s today, 35 percent for 80s, thirty percent for 70s, five percent for 60s. Rain is likely one year in three. A nighttime temperature in the 40s is possible now for the first time since the first week of July, a sign of the strength of the August 4th cool front, and a statistical step to autumn.

Natural Calendar

As Late Summer begins, all the katydids are singing. They call out the close of the Dog Days, and even though heat often lingers, the rhythm of the season has shifted, its tones have been altered, colors and sounds and scents all pointing to fall.

Now, almost everywhere in the country, average temperatures start to drop a degree and a half every seven days until the middle of September, at which point they decline about one degree every three days into January. Migration clucking among the robins increases. Some days, there will be a long and steady cardinal song before sunrise, then silence. Hummingbirds, wood ducks, Baltimore orioles and purple martins start to disappear south; their departure marks a quickening in the advent of Early Fall.

    Cottonwoods are yellowing. Black walnut foliage is thinning, foretaste of the great leafdrop to come. Locust leaves turn brown, damaged by leaf miners. Violet Joe Pye weed grays like thistledown. The prickly teasel dies back. Fruit of the bittersweet ripens. Spicebush berries redden. Tall goldenrod heads up. Rose pinks and great blue lobelia color the waysides. In the thunderstorms of Late Summer, green acorns and hickory nuts fall to the sweet rocket growing back among the budding asters. Spiders in the woods weave their final webs, and fireflies complete their cycle.

Daybook

1985: First boneset blooming at the frog pond near Grinnell Road. White snakeroot very early. First buds on the goldenrod. First yellow jacket seen.

1986: Only sporadic cardinal song today. No sparrows or robins. Grackles gone from the back trees.

1988: Mill Habitat: First white snakeroot. Jumpseed blooming, love vine gold now, covers the lizard's tail all along the river. A clump of showy coneflower, *rudbeckia speciosa*, is in full bloom by the dam.

1990: Jekyll Island, Georgia: Pennywort blooming, pokeweed berries half purple, half green, thick-leafed bindweed in bloom, varieties of trefoil with big, blue one-inch flowers, purslane, Virginia creepers, thorned greenbriar. Ragweed still not in bloom here.

1993: First bright blue dayflowers opened today. Through the village on my walks, a stability of purple coneflowers, violet mums, violet, white, and red phlox, golden coreopsis, showy coneflowers, tall coneflowers, bright zinnias and cosmos that will all last into September.

1997: This morning, the cardinals were loud at 5:00, but no robin chorus. That chorus is gone for the year now, ending with the last ten days or so of July. This afternoon into South Glen: One black walnut on the path. Early ironweed and wingstem. Blackberries mostly red. Wood nettle still full. Daddy longlegs do not have red eggs attached to their legs now. Full bloom of the oxeye. Cool breeze all day, the August 10th cold front arriving four days early.

1998: A cicada emerged last night on the back screen door, his old ecktoskeleton left hanging.

1999: Out for a walk along the Little Miami River: Virgin's bower, purple phlox, wingstem in bloom. In town, two resurrection lilies seen flowering. This afternoon, the first yellow jacket came to the fallen apples.

2002: At 5:40 a.m., only crickets heard, the whistling crickets and the chanting crickets. At 5:46, the first faint cardinals. Crows at 6:03, then doves almost immediately after. One jay call at 6:10.

2003: Five tiger swallowtails in the garden today. One black swallowtail was engaged in randori with them.

2005: Bud Marsh from Livermore Street called this afternoon to report at least half a dozen hummingbirds were swarming at his feeder. Although he remembered that the previous instance of this kind of end-of-summer clustering had taken place in September, a quick check of sources on the Internet suggests that this year Bud observed male hummingbirds as they were clustering for migration a month or so ahead of the females. In northern states, the male swarming can take place as early as July. Since Bud also saw hummingbird flocks in September, it is likely that those birds were females with their young, gorging themselves with sugar before their flight south. September 30 is an average date for the last hummingbird to leave Yellow Springs.

2006: The first ironweed buds were open this morning.

2007: Yellow leaves from the white mulberry, locust, and hackberry trees fall sporadically now in the breeze. The leafdrop has begun.

2008: To Portland, Oregon: Yellowing of a few trees along the Columbia River valley. Goldenrod prominent.

2010: Cardinal at 4:56, Crows at 5:23. Swallowtails, skippers, red admirals and monarchs continue as the sun reaches the butterfly bushes. Only six raspberries from the new patch today. Fallen black walnuts and apples in the alleyway.

2011: Portland, Oregon: Very little bird or insect song here in the suburbs, no flies, no mosquitoes, the land dry. Yucca in full bloom, mallow, Shasta daisies, some late wisteria, many lilies and large-flowered magnolias still have blossoms. Some blackberries ready to eat, some salmonberries red, soft, sweet.

2012: One loud cardinal outside my door at 5:03 this morning, robins already singing. In the garden, white bindweed flowers are multiplying. Many hosta leaves deep ochre. Heliopsis, phlox, knockout roses, one cluster of yellow tea rose blossoms, full showy coneflowers, an occasional reblooming lily (and Don has one lily plant still in full bloom), the faithful catmint, a few scraggly purple coneflowers (although Liz's and the ones in the Women's Park are still quite strong - but their petals fading), raggedy Shasta daisies, banks of zinnias providing almost all the color.

2013: Mateo's back lawn full of yellow leaves from the black walnut tree at the east edge of his property. At least three male tiger swallowtails in the yard today, always a female nearby. At Ellis Pond, the first arrowhead is blooming. From Vermont, Cathy writes: "It turned cold here yesterday. We had a thunderstorm and it hailed. Large pieces the size of peas covered the lawn and the deck. What a clatter! It feels like fall has come. Sweater time. Forecast says it will be in the 50s at night and 70s in the day. I saw several maples with leaves starting to turn, but maybe they were problem trees. Roadside weeds are turning beige. Fast forward climate change."

2014: Eight lily plants still have at least one blossom each. Moya's late-blooming, white-flowered hostas are almost ready to open, and the large hosta near our pond has substantial buds. A parent was feeding her fledgling sparrow in the honeysuckles, back and forth from the bird feeder every five to ten seconds, the young bird fluttering its wings almost the whole time. This afternoon, a large spicebush swallowtail came to the zinnias and stayed for about five minutes, sampling the different colors. I have been seeing the small golden skippers over the past week or so. Tonight was so loud with the static crickets and the high, steady crickets and a few field cricket chirps and the deafening katydids.

2015: Rain and cold all day, but cardinals singing throughout, starting a little after 5:00 – in spite of the fact that Jeanie used to say that the rain was about to stop when birds sang. I built a fire in the stove, closed the window to a chilly east wind. Six lilies at home. The Women's Park garden is still lush, but the golds and violets are fading just a little. Some coloring to a few serviceberry trees. Here, the zinnias, Joe Pye and the amaranth are drooping from the rain. Only the aggressive tithonias hold up – as they push out the other annuals.

2016: Walk with Jill, near Penn Yan, New York, a long path along the canal and then the river. Varied vegetation, most at the same level as in Yellow Springs. Joe Pye weed is fresh in full bloom here, Queen Anne's lace and purple loosestrife common, scattered heal-all, bouncing bets, one knotweed flower – but almost all the other knotweed plants not even budded. Black walnut leaves were starting to come down.

2017: Overcast, windless, misty and cool, a soft and quiet Sunday morning, secluded with honeysuckles, too early and dark for butterflies, the crickets screeching never pausing, cardinals competing with them, blue jay bell calls, crows,.
 Two bumblebees in the last bee balm flower, tiny, shining, gold and orange hoverflies exploring the arching stems of jumpseed full of small white blossoms, more hoverflies checking the seeds of old hostas and the rough leaves of the dark milkweed. The lone resurrection lily of the east garden had toppled over, broken at the base, and when I picked it up, and brought it to the

house and dropped it on the floor, half the brittle stalk just broke off.

A spined micrathena spider (a triangle of white and brown and black) in a wide web that stretched from a branch of forsythia to Janet's redbud tree, and another micrathena between Jeanie's redbud and a bamboo tree, both spiders returning to the center of their webs on guard when I approached, defiant against impossible odds. Spiders too in the studio where I study, house spiders I keep sweeping down with a broom and then they return in a few days, their webs rich with the ants that come inside.

Two fallen peaches, yellow-green, bruised and blotched: when I turned them over with my foot, I saw their undersides rotting dark orange and juicy. Rank pokeweed berries and healthy black and green milkweed pods fat, prickly and sticky beside the ailing peach tree.

Two mosquitoes side by side on my wrist, gone before I could look at them closely enough, but it seemed their legs were fringed with white. Sprouts of creeping Charlie growing up between my mossy patio bricks. Up the north side of the house the fearless, invading euonymus vines flowering in my face, and then the doe that lives between my house and Moya's emerged to eat the Anna Belle hydrangea, and then the fawn sidled in beside her, and I was all the things I saw.

2018: Three deer seen on a walk through the neighborhood, a mother and two fawns. Butterflies off and on throughout the day. The katydids started calling at 7:54 this evening, the earliest yet.

Nature is infinitely layered; the more an eager observer prepares for the seeing, the more Nature reveals of itself.

Peter London

August 7th
The 219th Day of the Year

But the flowers were now at their peak of blossom - Joe-Pye weed, last buttonball blooms, loosestrife, false boneset, many varieties of sunflowers, bouncing Bet – around which the sphinx moths foraged, wild balsam apples, milkweed, butterfly weed, bindweed, wild wisteria, self-heal, wood sage, hooded skullcap, wild bergamotte, monkey flowers, Beaumont's root, basilweed, and others.

August Derleth

Sunrise/set: 5:39/7:42
Day's Length: 14 hours 3 minutes
Average High/Low: 84/64
Average Temperature: 74
Record High: 97 – 1918
Record Low: 46 – 1889

Weather
Highs in the 90s come 20 percent of the days, in the 80s sixty percent, in the 70s twenty percent. Rain falls one year out of five. Totally overcast conditions occur just 15 percent of the years. Cool lows in the 50s are recorded 15 percent of the years, too.

Natural Calendar
The end of fireflies, the occasional long and loud robin valediction song, the first yellow jackets in the windfall apples and peaches and plums, the appearance of red stonecrop, white snakeroot, and boneset flowers, the fading of the cottonwoods, the occasional falling black walnut leaf and a vague scent of fall combine now with all the other endings and beginnings to accelerate the year, building momentum with an accumulation of more and more events.

Daybook

1983: Orton Path: The tree line is turning ever so slightly, a hint of tan and yellow in the black walnuts. Air heavy with the sweet, honey-like smell of corn pollen. Only a few teasel flowers, a few yarrow left, some daisy fleabane, a few white sweet clover. Field thistle, burdock, pokeweed, heal-all, leaf cup, mullein, tall bellflower, false foxglove, lopseed, and wild lettuce are in full bloom. White snakeroot opening. A great blue heron flew overhead as I walked; it turned and banked over Clifton Gorge then disappeared into the forest. Blackberries full fruit now. First Asiatic dayflowers blooming in the yard.

1986: First geese of the year flew over at 6:14 a.m. To the Little Miami at 10:00, fishing with dough balls: A few bites, no fish. I stretched out on the bank of the river. I lay smelling the pollen from corn and sunflowers, watching swallowtails mating in the sycamore above me, tracking the wind whenever it marked the surface of the water, listening to the heavy pulse of cicada song, imagining the whole field at Middle Prairie full of golden coneflowers and purple ironweed.

1987: Cottonwood leaves yellowing, the tree line turning just a little.

1993: Red and violet phlox begin their decline, but the whites, which opened later, are in full bloom. Some patches of purple coneflowers are fading in the village. The ones in the east garden are still at their peak. Only a handful of fireflies seen tonight.

1996: August sedum, with its pale purple flowers, is open in town now. At the corner of Dayton-Yellow Springs Road and Highway 235, there is a three-foot smart weed in bloom -- or a pink-flowered dock - a volunteer this year brought in by the floods in April and May. It has long, straight pink flowers and large alternate leaves. Probably a *Polygonum coccineum* - swamp smartweed.

1997: Our generic midseason hostas are gone now, all but a few petals.

1998: Robin singsong at 5:10 a.m. Yellow yarrow fades now.

1999: The yard is full of butterflies today: cabbage whites and silver-spotted skippers at the purple loosestrife (which has made a comeback in the last week), yellow swallowtails, black swallowtails. Blue-tailed darners at the pond. Geese flew over the house about 6:00 this morning, first time I've heard them this year (and the same day and time as in 1986).

2000: The rate of change accelerates, as does the shift in my mood. To what extent am I susceptible to the new deeper colors of the leaves, the trickle of leaves into the undergrowth, to the aging of the garden, the multiplication of butterflies? I believe I am protected by my social context and my economic status and my work and family concerns, but those things insulate me less from the environment than from being honest with myself. The tangle of self-analysis itself is a sign of fall; I can't answer the questions, can't settle the restlessness, and so I daydream and mark time.

2001: Walk at 5:00 a.m., third quarter moon setting in the southwest, Jupiter a finger's width away from Venus in the east, cardinals and robins singing, the last katydids of the night at 5:14, a screech owl at 5:17.

2002: The Royal Standard hosta began to bloom today.

2003: No birds this morning until cardinals started to sing at about 5:15. The last of the Turk's cap lilies fell today.

2004: I noticed a small toad in the garden this afternoon. Have the snakes moved elsewhere? Far fewer snakes seen near the pond this summer.

2005: Four monarchs seen on the Joe Pye plant this afternoon. Tiger and spicebush swallowtails common. Only four lily plants still have one or more flowers.

2006: A cardinal called this morning at 4:59 a.m. and continued through dawn. Whistling crickets were singing from the time I got up until daylight. Only one dove heard about 5:20. Cicadas strong from sunup on. Lindy called from Antioch School: a wren's nest with four blue eggs inside found in a bookshelf in her room. Only three daylilies left in bloom today on three separate plants. The Resurrection lilies, however, remain strong. Some bi-color-leafed hostas have stayed in full bloom. A flock of house sparrows has been feeding in the yard all afternoon, especially in the rose of Sharon, as though something has hatched and is providing a good meal for them. Monarchs and black swallowtails seen this afternoon. First Royal Standard hosta blossom today, like in 2002.

2007: Resurrection lilies, giant hibiscus, rose of Sharon, white-flowered August hostas (in Moya's yard), showy coneflowers, great ragweed, tall coneflowers, purples coneflowers, black-eyed Susans, thin-leafed coneflowers, gray-headed coneflowers, Joe Pye weed are all in full bloom. Heliopsis continues bright, but the lower heliopsis with bi-colored leaves is dying back now. Daisy fleabane continues to flower, has not let up since June.

2010: Robin chorus in the dark when I went out at 4:40 this morning. A cardinal sang at 4:55. Two tiger swallowtails, two red admirals, two spicebush swallowtails, two monarchs seen today.

2011: Portland, Oregon: Wheat fields in the hills around the city are golden brown but still with a faint tint of yellow green. In Jeni's back yard, rose of Sharon bushes are budded like in Yellow Springs June.

2012: Static-like sound from tree crickets, whistling crickets (high and steady), chirping field crickets, and intermittent buzzing crickets in the evenings. This morning, robins broke through the cricket racket at 5:10, and cardinals and doves came in by 5:25. A few monarchs and swallowtails noticed throughout the day.

2013: Crows at 5:48 this morning. Black walnut leaves starting to appear in the school park. Three male tiger swallowtails and one female in the butterfly bushes around 8:30 this morning. No monarchs seen so far this year.

2014: Six lily plants still have at least one blossom. The phlox remain an important anchor for the central line of the north garden, the low, blue spiderwort – blooming since June – continues to complement the tall, violet phlox. A fleeting glimpse of either a viceroy or a great spangled fritillary at noon. At 3:30, a giant swallowtail in the zinnias. In the arboretum at Ellis Pond, the autumn change is quickly taking place: black walnut leaves are yellowing, a dogwood has patches of red, so many trees now rusted and shaggy with age. Tree crickets very loud (static and high trills) from dusk through the night, katydids starting at 8:05 sharp. From Goshen, Indiana, Judy (on her birthday) writes: "On a Sunday walk in the woods, we saw little toads hopping about, more than we usually see in three or four walks."

2015: Six lily plants, ten blossoms in all. Male and female tiger swallowtails throughout the day, small golden skippers, silver-spotted skippers, one monarch. In the yard and about town, the variegated hostas have just about completed their seasons. The Royal Standard hosta by the pond has started to open. The north gardens, the most complex of the plantings I have, need additional sequence plantings for August, perhaps more coneflowers. Along the town roads, some cottonwood leaves have yellowed.

2016: Return from Penn Yan and Keuka Lake in New York: Along the freeway west, bright roadsides of silver Queen Anne's lace, sky-blue chicory, yellow sow thistles. Many cornfields stressed from drought. At home, the Joe Pye has started to turn brown, a few phlox flowers remaining, zinnias and tithonias continuing to give color to the garden, some rose of Sharon. A lone peach, the very last of the dying peach tree, was on the ground. I picked it up to save for planting. Some second-bloom violet blossoms on the wisteria. No lilies at all. In the dark, raucous katydids and screeching crickets.

2017: More peaches coming down, along with a few leaves, the leaf drop picking up. The Royal Standard hostas under the apple tree are fully budded, and Jill's blue vervain has just started to flower. Only cabbage white butterflies seen in the garden today.

2018: Monarch, silver-spotted skippers and tiger swallowtail sightings continue. Five cabbage whites seen playing near the Joe Pye plants, the first time I've seen so many together this summer.

Go where he will, the wise man is at home,
His hearth the earth, his hall the azure dome;
Where his clear spirit leads him, there's his road,
By God's own light illumined and foreshowed.

Ralph Waldo Emerson

August 8th
The 220th Day of the Year

The air sizzles with insect song. Crickets and grasshoppers warn and wook, rubbing their musical legs. They make the sound of beans rolling in a pan, tiny bells ringing on the ankles of dancers, fingers raked over the teeth of combs, waves rolling cobbles on the shore.

Scott Russell Sanders

Sunrise/set: 5:40/7:41
Day's Length: 14 hours 1 minute
Average High/Low: 84/64
Average Temperature: 74
Record High: 99 – 1901
Record Low: 49 – 1889

Weather

Today's highs are in the 90s thirty-five percent of all the years, in the 80s forty-five percent of the time, 70s the remainder of the years. The chance of rain is 20 percent. Sun dominates. Conditions may be unsettled, however, as a cool front typically passes through Ohio between today and the 12th. Chilly nights in the 40s come 15 percent of the years.

The Weather in the Week Ahead

This week's highs: 50 percent of the afternoons are in the 80s, 25 percent in the 90s and another 25 percent in the 70s. Rainfall is typically light, with the 9th, 12th, 13th, and 14th carrying just a ten to 15 percent chance of a shower. With the arrival of the August 10th cold front, however, the 10th and 11th have a 40 percent chance of precipitation as well as the slight possibility of a high only in the 60s for the first time since July 13th. The 10th through the 14th are likely to bring evening lows below 60 degrees. And within the next seven days, lows reach into the 40s fifteen times more often than they do during the first week of August.

The Natural Calendar

Everbearing strawberries and watermelons ripen; summer apples are half picked, and tobacco is often topped on two out of three of all the plots along the Ohio River. Peaches are at their best throughout the Midwest. The first soybeans are turning, and most are setting pods. The harvest of winter wheat and oats is complete throughout the nation. Farmers bring in corn for silage, dig potatoes, pick tomatoes and finish the second cut of alfalfa hay. This is the beginning of lawn seeding time, and the time for band seeding alfalfa on the farm. Smooth brome grass, orchard grass and timothy are also planted now.

The Stars

Winter's Orion and the Summer Triangle are balanced and connected by the Milky Way. Each pulls the other to its appointed place, keeping perfect equilibrium, compressing the year into a cycle visible on the small, round dome of heaven.

Orion is the easy gauge of winter, rising with the Milky Way on November evenings, filling the southern sky throughout the night all winter, finally disappearing late in April. As Orion waxes, all of the pieces of summer recede; as that constellation wanes, each piece returns.

The Summer Triangle is the stellar gauge of summer. It is a parallel marker to Orion that clocks the unfolding of the leaves and flowers. Accompanied by the opposite end of the Milky Way, it appears on the evenings of May. Its triple constellations, Lyra, Cygnus and Aquila, contain three prominent capstone stars, Vega, Deneb and Altair, which form a giant triangle.

When all these stars come up after dark, the canopy of leaves is complete. Mock orange and peonies and iris blossom in the gardens of the Ohio Valley morning birdsong swells, strawberries ripen, sweet clover is open by the roadsides, and goslings enter adolescence along the rivers.

When Vega, Deneb and Altair are positioned overhead at midnight, then the birds are quiet, ragweed pollen is in the air, blackberries are sweet, hickory nuts and black walnuts are falling, katydids and cicadas and late crickets are singing, rose of Sharon colors the garden.

When leaves are turning all along the 40th Parallel and the last wildflowers have completed their cycles, then Lyra, Cygnus and Aquila set in the west after sundown, leading the Milky Way through Cassiopeia and Perseus, dividing the heavens into equal halves, for an instant holding in balance summer and winter, linking the Summer Triangle with Orion rising again in the east.

Daybook

1984: Virgin's bower and Japanese knotweed blooming along the railroad tracks near the Children's Center, velvetleaf in the soybean fields.

1986: Color shift beginning along the tracks, milkweed yellows by the roadsides.

1988: Jacoby: Avens gone to burs, early white snakeroot, ragweed early full, oxeye full, spider webs across the way every few yards (peak of spider webs now), tall bellflower late, tall coneflower full, trumpet creeper holding, last of the white vervain, teasel dying back, fresh four-inch red thorns on the locust, rough bedstraw full, blue vervain seven feet high and full bloom, purple ironweed, too.

1990: Home from Florida to loud city crickets and katydids that started up while I was gone.

1992: Long and steady cardinal song before dawn, then silence.

1993: At South Glen, the wood nettle is about half gone now, leaves tattered, seeds beginning to form. Blackberries are early full for picking. Most wingstem and ironweed still not fully developed.

1996: The pieces of Late Summer fall into place. The heat stays, but the rhythm has shifted, the tones have been altered, colors and sounds and scents all pointing to September. The katydids, which started to sing last week, are in full chorus after dark. The cicadas have finally all come out and fill the afternoons. The town geese have delayed their restless flights in the cool summer, but they should start moving back and forth across town any day. The smell of the wind is becoming more pungent, sweeter, sharper as the vegetation evolves.

1997: The last of the day lilies and Asiatic lilies.

1998: The Royal Standard hostas are in full bloom now in the yard and around town.

1999: Hummingbird still coming to the rose of Sharon at 6:00 in the morning. Honeysuckle berries green, half size. Purple butterfly bush and loosestrife have both recovered from their July slump, are blooming strong. Several cottonwoods turning along the freeway, one Judas maple yellow-orange, a black walnut tree here in town.

2000: By this point in the year, so many of the notations in my natural history journal point toward fall. The notes and the actual changes accumulate until summer disappears, and a new season of new pieces emerges.

2001: Royal Standard hosta: one in full bloom, tall stems with large white trumpet flowers, one budded.

2003: No birds until 5:15 a.m. First blue Asiatic dayflower bloomed at the northwest corner of the house this morning.

2004: Greg called, said he saw a green cicada emerging today. I noticed a new green cicada on the back arbor the other day, didn't realized it had just come out of its shell – which was a few feet away. These are late-emerging annuals. About town, several more Judas maples are turning.

2005: Cardinals began singing at 5:00 a.m., gathered momentum for half an hour, then quieted to sporadic through the day. Crescent-spot butterfly found on the showy coneflowers this afternoon; it remained there for at least an hour while I searched to match its markings in my butterfly book. Monarchs and tiger swallowtails and spicebush swallowtails continue abundant in the garden.

2006: Katydids still sang until 4:40 a.m. First cardinal at 4:59. The black walnut tree in the school park has lost maybe a third of its leaves.

2007: The last lily in the yard has wilted. Some euonymus flowers turning to berries. Several branches on the southwest redbud seem to have died, foliage withered. One dead branch also on Janet's redbud.

2010: Cardinal heard at 5:05, robin singsong when I went outside at 5:20. Tiger swallowtails all day, a few monarchs. Driving in to Dayton, we saw pale Judas maples, blanching sections of cottonwoods, yellowing milkweed leaves.

2011: Portland, Oregon: Linden tree fruits dropping, crunching as we walked the suburbs this afternoon. No insect song throughout the day and night, only occasional crows and a few other calls unrecognized.

2012: Some turning of the maple trees noticed on our drive into Dayton this morning, the changes complementing the slight yellowing of the cottonwoods. In the alley, small-flowered coneflowers and Mrs. Timberlakes's feverfew are in full bloom, but the tall coneflower plants never appeared this year, were probably pulled up.

2013: Warm, humid, rain and sun. Three male tiger swallowtails in the butterfly bushes again. One yellow lily in the circle garden is the only one left.

2014: Six lily plants in bloom, thanks to the naked lady and two rebloomers. A tiger swallowtail sitting in the river birch this morning. Moya's drift of August hostas has just started to open. Judy's, a few houses down the street, have been open several days. Two more tiger swallowtails, a black swallowtail (or spicebush) and a monarch around town this afternoon.

2015: I was outside too late to hear the first cardinal song, but one was warming up at 4:55 a.m. Seven lily plants today, close to last year. Three monarchs and many swallowtails, skippers and whites in the yard today. Sun and color in the garden, warm but not too humid, perfect time for butterflies. Cardinal vespers 6:00 – 6:30 p.m.

2016: A field cricket in the kitchen this morning when I came out to make coffee. No naked ladies came up in the east garden this year. Buds beginning on the New England asters Butterflies: numerous silver-spotted skippers, a giant swallowtail, a male tiger swallowtail, a great spangled fritillary.

2017: A cool wind throughout the day. Cabbage whites, a few blues in the garden midmorning. A little later, a hackberry brown came and bumped me on the back of my head, and then on my shoulder, and then sat on my forearm. She had emerged, perhaps, to tend the fallen peaches near the huge hackberry tree. I greeted her as Jeanie. This afternoon, a giant swallowtail in the zinnias, then four yellow tiger swallowtails, then a black swallowtail and another hackberry brown, and as I sat watching the zinnias, hummingbirds came and went, and golden fold-winged skippers played in the ferns by my side, and cabbage whites chased each other the length of the garden.

2018: Cabbage whites mating in the Joe Pye plants. One monarch and one male yellow swallowtail spent much of the day in the garden. The first peach fell from Neysa's peach tree. The last Stargazer lily faded yesterday. This evening, the katydids began to call at exactly 7:56.

There comes a fuzzy time then, when the berry picking mixes with the end of hay gathering and the beginning of Late Summer and everything seems to fall into a stew. Dog days, when the dog literally will not move from beneath the porch and the weather come down hot and muggy so the teams of horses stand in sweat even then they are not working.

Gary Paulsen

August 9th
The 221st Day of the Year

Now comes the time of rich purple in the fields and meadows, denoting not only a time but also a maturity. It is as though the whole Summer had been building toward this deep, strong color to match the gold of late sunlight and early goldenrod.

Hal Borland

Sunrise/set: 5:41/7:40
Day's Length: 13 hours 59 minutes
Average High/Low: 84/64
Average Temperature: 74
Record High: 99 – 1894
Record Low: 49 – 1884

Weather
Today is one of the sunniest of all the August days, with a 90 percent chance of clear to partly cloudy skies. Showers pass through the Lower Midwest 15 percent of the time. Hot temperatures in the 90s occur 25 percent of the afternoons, and 80s come on 50 percent, 70s on 20 percent. There is a five percent chance of an afternoon high only in the 60s.

Natural Calendar
The day's length shortens more quickly as August progresses. At solstice, the night was around nine hours in length along the 40th Parallel. By today, after six weeks of Middle Summer, the night has grown to ten hours. Now, it takes a little more than three weeks to grow by another hour.

Daybook
1982: First maple leaves yellow in Goes Station three miles south of town.

1986: Geese flew over at 6:30 a.m. and 6:30 p.m. The first patch of yellow appeared on the big maple in the yard. Tree of heaven fading. Clearweed noticed blooming. A few fireflies seen tonight.

1988: Fireflies, delayed by the drought, have actually increased tonight over a month ago.

1993: The last daylily opened this morning. Blue vervain on the Miller's land was just starting its climb to autumn.

1996: Cottonwoods becoming pale yellow at a number of locations in the area. At the mill habitat, black walnut, sumac, wild grape, sycamore, elm, box elder, and redbud are also turning yellow along the river. One Virginia creeper on a fallen log was red. This morning, I saw a shower of yellow leaves fall into the garden, box elders. Coming home from downtown, we watched the wren in the front maple scolding Jerome, the cat.

1998: The maple in front of our house has started to turn now, one of the earliest of the local Judas trees. Many cottonwoods are blanching quickly. Along the highways, sundrops, ironweed, false boneset, wingstem are in full bloom. Katydids started at 8:02 p.m. along Jacoby road as Jeanie and I were walking back from the river.

1999: Brief robin song this morning around nine o'clock, for just a minute or so, then silence. A half an hour later, a huge gray toad appeared at the pond, skin hanging around his flanks as though he had just lost half his weight.

2000: Crickets when I got up this morning: a single shrill call, unwavering. Cardinal at 5:11, several of them sang until almost 6:00. Cloudy, humid and windless morning. Pink and white phlox, heliopsis declining. Mallow almost all gone. Purple loosestrife just about done. Showy coneflowers are in the middle of their season, all in bloom, none fading. When the sky grew dark and a storm moved in, a blue jay in the back yard gave warning with its bell call, maybe a dozen cries before the wind struck.

2001: Cardinal at 5:09 a.m., crows at 5:21, blue jay then a squirrel at 5:25. A warm quiet morning, moon three quarters full, predawn sky dusky blue, Jupiter starting to move up and away from Venus in the east, ending conjunction.

2006: Katydids had become silent when I got up this morning at about 1:00. No sound either at about 3:30 or at 4:30. A few isolated "katy-dids" just before a cardinal sang at 4:56. Skunk odor drifting over from Stafford Street about 5:30. In the alley, lilac seeds elongating. All of Mrs. Timberlake's phlox and lilies are gone. Jeanie and I sat on the porch about 7:15, the weather cloudy and cool. Male and female hummingbirds came to the feeder, but no butterflies in the yard. No cicadas because of the clouds and temperature, only a few cardinal calls. Only one lily is left blooming in the yard, a red-orange. In the pond, arrowhead has started to bloom.

2007: Robins strong this morning near 5:00 a.m. The cardinals sang a few times, and I heard one crow about 6:30, but no early doves.

2010: Faint robinsong, loud crickets at 4:40. One cardinal at 4:45, then quiet until about 5:00. Tiger swallowtails and monarchs continue – and later today, a silvery zebra swallowtail, a fritillary and two Eastern Black Swallowtails. Tat said last night that the monarchs in Madison had been abundant this summer. I noticed a patch of gold forming on the front ash tree; a large branch of the white mulberry has bright yellow leaves. Across the street, Lil's burning bush has blushed across the top.

2012: Robins and cardinals singing when I checked at 5:15 this morning. A small skunk appeared out of the darkness to run across our back porch about 5:30. Late-season hostas in bloom at Moya's and along the west border of the yard. Shasta daisies almost gone here, stronger at Liz's garden. Phlox holding. Goldenrod is fully headed at the Danielsons', but not as far advanced as I would have thought with all the heat. Two male tiger swallowtails at one time this afternoon in the butterfly bush, and occasional spicebush swallowtails.

2013: Two pale yellow lilies in the circle garden and along the north garden. Other lilies – mostly orange tiger lilies – still flowering in the village. Phlox past the height of their bloom. Some roses, but the lack of fertilizer and late trimming pretty much ended their season after the first wave of blooms. Butterfly bushes hold. Shasta daisies still strong. Tiger swallowtails, male and female, along with a giant swallowtail visited the flowers today. As I walked to the east gate, I was surprised to see that one of our resurrection lilies was in the bloom. (They had not flowered in years.) Properly situated, those pale violet lilies follow closely after the disappearance of standard lilies.

2014: Five lilies in bloom (counting the naked lady and the last stargazer). One monarch seen in the north garden zinnias at about 10:00 a.m. Another in the afternoon.

2015: This morning, I was there for the first cardinal song, 4:49. In the middle of the cricket symphony: the soft chirping of the field crickets, the intermittent trill of the tree crickets (the whistling crickets), the static of the thrips.

2016: First cardinals at 5:05 this morning. Chirping field crickets, high static of thrips. No robins. Crows at 6:10. Butterflies: two giant swallowtails, several male tiger swallowtails, two faded Eastern Blacks, one monarch, one spicebush swallowtail. Shasta daisies and helianthus are well past their best now, many cut back, purple coneflower color faded almost to gray, Joe Pye still strong. The powdery-pink naked ladies are in full flower along Elm Street.

2017: A hackberry brown enjoying a fallen peach this morning, feeding, flitting, settling back to feed some more. More fold-wing skippers and cabbage whites in randori. One small black swallowtail in the zinnias this afternoon. At Ellis Pond, the bullfrog is still calls at sundown.

2018: Eight cabbage whites clustering around the jumpseed clump, one monarch, one male tiger swallowtail in the zinnias in the morning, two monarchs together in the afternoon, two question marks, several silver-spotted skippers. The first goldenrod seen in bloom near Wright Street. Yellowing hackberry leaves continue to fall, a major early leaf shedding. The description of the daisies and coneflowers and naked ladies from 2016 fits today perfectly. Katydids a little before 8:00 this evening.,

The earth is good, and the changing seasons are a joy.

Harlan Hubbard

August 10th
The 222nd Day of the Year

Tall ironweed blooms
All around us, purple-blue clusters
Blazing atop stalks six feet tall....

Ann Filemyr

Sunrise/set: 5:42/7:38
Day's Length: 13 hours 56 minutes
Average High/Low: 84/64
Average Temperature: 74
Record High: 99 – 1900
Record Low: 49 – 1972

Weather

Today is one of the most decisive days in the decline of Middle Summer. The chances of 90-degree temperatures, which have remained fairly steady between 30 and 45 percent since the beginning of July, abruptly fall to between 15 and 20 percent. Completely cloudy conditions occur 30 percent of the years; chances of highs in the cool 70s are 25 percent, and chances of rain increase to 40 percent. Average temperatures have come down just one degree since July 28th, the date when the stability of Middle Summer began to deteriorate. Starting today, averages drop a degree and a half per week until September 10th, when they decline one degree every three days into January.

Natural Calendar

In forests and fields, touch-me-nots are still in full bloom, tall bellflowers strong and blue, burdock holding beside the oxeye, bouncing bets and new six-petaled wild cucumbers, the yellow and the blue flowered wild lettuce, the bull thistle, virgin's bower, tall nettle, prickly mallow, small woodland sunflower, soft velvetleaf, sundrops and heal all in full flower.

Along the rivers, bur marigolds, zigzag goldenrod, and broad-leafed swamp goldenrod are budding. Water horehound, willow herb, wood mint and swamp milkweed are still open. Late Summer's jumpseeds are not ready to jump yet. Damselflies still hunt by the water. Cabbage butterflies still mate.

Daybook

1984: Early morning: A huge imperial moth on the outside wall of the Earth Rose store downtown. On the road east, goldenrod early full bloom from a few miles out of Columbus, but none in Yellow Springs. Through Pennsylvania, the same roadside flowers as in Greene County: Sundrops, Queen Anne's lace, chicory, Joe Pye, ironweed, wingstem full bloom.

1985: Outer Banks, North Carolina: I sat beside the pennywort and fingered its seeds, stroked its round leaves. I walked through the sea oats to the top of the dunes and looked out at the waves. Ghost crabs scavenged in the shells and debris of the beach. The sky was so clear and blue. The sun and the wind pushed together on my back with a firm, hot pressure.

1986: Cardinals even quieter now. Black walnut trees losing their leaves. Locusts browning at Wilberforce. Poplars shifting color.

1989: The morning is quiet, only doves calling in the back woods, and a wren in the rose of Sharon north of the garden. Five or six apples fell from the tree in the past hour, muffled, uneven strokes of Late Summer's pendulum.

1991: Patches of red Virginia creeper, orange dodder growing across the wild raspberries. Yellow jackets drawn to the fallen apples this week, lilies and trumpet creepers declining, fireflies almost gone, new green acorns on the path, just before katydids, the first flocks of geese fly over town, blackberries in at South Glen, bittersweet, heavy air, the scent of fall.

1996: Golden and purple coneflowers, and red, pink and violet phlox dominate the gardens of Yellow Springs now. A clavate tortoise beetle found on one of the tomato plants today, a small, odd brown beetle truly similar in appearance to a tortoise. When I was paging through the insect identification book, the beetle got away from me, and I lost him in the grass. I looked all over the tomatoes and weeds to see if I could find another, but no luck. This evening around 6:30, I was eating downtown with Jeanie when to the south, near Glen Helen, the first geese of August flew over, calling.

1998: Robin singsong about 5:15 this morning, crows about 5:30, cardinals near 6:00.

2000: Two lily blooms left. The yard silent at 6:25 this morning except for a blue jay in the honeysuckles. Tonight, with the moon almost full over the south garden, the soft descending whinny of a screech owl in the back trees. The bird called for maybe three or four minutes, then ceded to katydids.

2001: Yellow yarrow cut back today. Phlox deteriorating quickly in the heat, victim of powdery mildew, the rain and old age. Arrowhead bloomed over night in the pond.

2002: A cool morning in the 50s, dew on the grass, the scent of apples and old leaves in the air.

2005: Heat wave continues, 15-plus days over 90 so far this summer. Lilies are down to only three blossoms today. Along the roads, cottonwoods are developing yellow leaves, locusts have patches of brown, some silver olive shrubs show yellow. Webworms, cut last week from the apple tree, have reappeared.

2006: After a cooling, light rain, the katydids refused to sing last night. This morning, fog covers the village. In the alley, Mateo's black walnut has lost about half its leaves. Euonymus full bloom, tall coneflowers full, but the first blossom has lost its petals. Sparrows continue to move in small flocks through the undergrowth.

2010: The last of the orange day lilies – the plants that have outlasted all the other lilies by more than two weeks are set to open their last blossoms today. At 5:00 this morning, robins and cardinals were in full song, the humidity high, temperature almost 75.

2012: Robins still singsonging in the mornings, cardinals quieter. The first day in 70s in what seems like all summer, the August 10th cool front arriving right on schedule.

2013: No robins, but steady cardinal song through the neighborhood at 5:15 this morning. Only one dove heard in the distance at 5:30. Tiger swallowtails, male and female, and skippers at the butterfly bush this noon.

2014: Cardinals all around the block at 5:05 this morning, probably started earlier. No robins heard. Eight lilies in bloom, a dozen blossoms in all.

2016: Cardinals in song a little after 5:00 as in previous years, no robins. Three Stella d'oro blossoms. Lil's burning bush foliage has a blush of red. Small skippers and at least one male tiger swallowtail when the sun broke through the storms. Two prairie dock flowers are open on the High Street/West South College Street corner.

2017: A monarch was visiting the zinnias and the Joe Pye weed this noon. Two hackberry butterflies noticed by the peach tree. Fold-wing skippers and cabbage whites common this afternoon. Jonatha reports sighting two more monarchs for a total of three so far this summer.

2018: Many cabbage whites, a silver-spotted skipper and a monarch in the zinnias. Two yellow ever-blooming lilies are open, jumpseed is in full flower, attracting cabbage whites. Winterberry full, too. And Royal Standard hostas. During the night, deer had eaten off two tomato plants, and under the trellis, I found a fawn with spots sleeping soundly, escaped from the noise of the house construction on the other side of the honeysuckles.

We listen to the spaces between the sounds of the birds and insects, watch the spaces between seasonal corners, and then between our feelings and our dreams.

      Eliades Quintana

August 11th
The 223rd Day of the Year

But I shall see the August weather spur
Berries to ripen where the flowers were—
Dark berries, savage-sweet and worth the wait—
And there will come the moment to be quick
And save some from the birds, and I shall need
Two pails, old clothes in which to stain and bleed,
And a grandchild to talk with while we pick.

Richard Wilbur

Sunrise/set: 5:43/7:37
Day's Length: 13 hours 54 minutes
Average High/Low: 84/63
Average Temperature: 74
Record High: 98 – 1900
Record Low: 48 – 1890

Weather

There is a 50 percent chance of rain today, but the sun comes out seven years in ten. Most afternoons are in the 80s, but there is a 20 percent chance of 90s, fifteen percent for 70s, and ten percent for a high only in the 60s. Evenings cool into the 50s half of the years. Today is the traditional last date for the "Dog Days" in most almanacs.

Natural Calendar

August is the month in which the Judas trees show their color, bright orange in the otherwise sold green of maples. It is the time that catalpas start to wear thin, and showers of black walnut leaves foretell autumn. Saplings are browning under the high canopy. Patches of scarlet have appeared in the sumac and poison ivy.

In perennial gardens, the last red, white, and violet phlox, golden and purple coneflowers, bright helianthus and pale resurrection lilies define Late Summer. Along the highways, beds of false boneset have come into bloom beside the July drifts of blue chicory and silver Queen Anne's lace.

Wild plums are ripe for jam, and woodland grapes are purple. Some elderberries are ready for wine. Puffball mushrooms emerge among spring's rotting stems and leaves when the evenings are cool. Greenbriar fruits darken. Orange bittersweet berries are sometimes mature and ready to pick.

Morning fogs thicken as the night air cools. Crickets, cicadas and katydids become more insistent. Webworms emerge from their Late Summer webs. Grackle activity increases while cardinal song becomes fainter. The early morning robins are silent. Long flocks of blackbirds pursue the harvest. Sparrow flocks grow larger. Starlings swoop in murmurations. Whip-poor-wills, cedar waxwings and catbirds follow the signs to the Gulf of Mexico. In the wetlands of the Southeast, alligators hatch from their eggs, and cottonmouth snakes give birth to their young.

Daybook

1982: Day lilies gone now.

1983: Maple along Dayton Street pale yellow. Some poplar leaves bright yellow. The smell of the wind is changing, becoming more pungent, sweeter, sharper.

1986: Buckeyes hanging heavy on the branches, and leaves rusty around the edges. Robins clucking through the day, no longer chirping and chanting in the early morning, Joe Pye weed fading, lopseed and panicled tick trefoil late bloom, early white snakeroot, red leaves of Virginia creeper and some sumac, green acorns on the path, first great blue lobelia found, skunk cabbage decayed, and the swamp littered with its stalks. First goldenrod discovered blooming at High Prairie. Asiatic bittersweet berries are yellow gold, along the fence: I broke off a branch of them, put it in my notebook; the hulls were open by morning. Geese flew over this evening at 8:02 p.m.

1988: Cardinals still singing all day. Did the drought delay part of their cycle?

1991: Cardinals, doves, flicker, robins, grackles loud in the early morning. Geese flew over at 8:41 a.m.

1993: First autumn fog this morning all the way south into Xenia. The very last day lily in the yard is blooming today; some gardens in the village have a few more, and it may be another week before the very last domestic day lily is gone. Two alypia moths found today, one at home, one eight miles away near my office. This is the first time I've noticed these small black creatures with their pale spotted wings. I feel like I've stumbled onto a secret.

1996: Cloudy and cool today, the August 10th cold front settling in. A cardinal sang from early morning on, debunking all my notes on quiet August birds. The first raspberries are coming in today in our bedraggled berry patch.

1997: First Judas maple seen along Dayton Street yesterday, cottonwoods, black walnuts, locusts yellowing in patches about town, too, just as the first pink stonecrop sedum blooms at the corner of High Street and Dayton Street.

1999: Every lily is gone now. Ten cabbage butterflies at the loosestrife. A new brood?

2000: Natural history can be a litany of turning points in the progress of the year, and the motion of the Earth around the Sun produces more such points than I ever imagined. Each day brings out more turns and corners in the apparently straight, uniform field of the season. I can rest momentarily, find the elusive present in the color and sound of the spaces between those corners.

2004: The first cardinal in the neighborhood sang at exactly 5:10 this morning. Doves came in at 5:25. The crescent moon was high in the east, a palm's width above Venus.

2005: The worst storm since August 27, 2003 came in this afternoon with blinding, horizontal rain, thunder and lightning. A great branch from the white mulberry in back came down, bringing half of the remaining branches of the tallest locust. Our redbuds and one hydrangea damaged.

2007: Phlox have dwindled to maybe a fifth of their full bloom, and a rapid decline of all July blossoms. Japanese beetles have returned to the roses, destroyed the tea roses over night, left the bush roses alone. Purple coneflowers declining, as yellow coneflowers become the staple of village gardens. Bi-color-leafed hydrangeas continue to flower along the north wall garden. False boneset fully budded. Arrowhead is in full bloom along the west edge of the pond. No sign of flowers on the virgin's bower here or along Elm Street.

2008: Left Portland, Oregon today for Baker City east of the Columbia River gorge and down towards Boise. The past week in Oregon has been hectic, and my mental notes have been sporadic. Jeni picked blackberries at Rooster Rock park, and the fruit was dark and sweet; in other parts of the area, though, there were blackberry flowers and green fruit. At the Portland zoo, oakleaf hydrangea petals were still white, and late monarda was holding, a sign of the delayed summer here close to the 45th Parallel. Fireweed, moth mullein, goldenrod were other familiar markers throughout the area. Across eastern Oregon, harvest of rich brown grains continues; some fresh, green alfalfa seen growing; this is cattle country – hay and grazing land seem to be the staples of the countryside.

2010: Robins at 5:00, the chorus continuing, the singsong kept up all day. Male and female tiger swallowtails, Eastern black swallowtails, Monarchs in the garden today. Across the countryside, wingstem and ironweed in full bloom along the roads, soybeans deep green, corn lush. Neysa called from Italy, said they would be camping to watch the Lagrimas de San Lorenzo meteors, the Perseids. More robin vespers this evening.

2011: Portland, Oregon: Wheat harvest starting, crows calling, no insect sounds in the city, only two songbirds heard in a week here, only two cabbage white butterflies, weather clear, warm and dry.

2012: Morning robin chorus still going on around 5:00 a.m.

2013: To Madison, Wisconsin: Fog spread across the fields as I started out in the early morning. All the usual wildflowers through the freeway drive: Queen Anne's lace, trefoil, chicory (opening about two hours past sunrise), orange trumpet creepers, Joe Pye, white-flowered teasel, crown vetch, sundrops, false boneset, ironweed, sow thistles, white and pink bindweed blossoms, some stonecrop. Wild cucumber plants common, their white flowers and vines climbing the hedgerows throughout the Midwest. No red-winged blackbirds on the fences. Great mullein flowering only at the very tips of their stalks. Some milkweed leaves yellowing. Prairie dock and compass plant seen in Illinois. Three monarchs on the wing. Signs of returning to Middle Summer: drifts of daisy fleabane, and white sweet clover and orange ditch lilies near Rockford, a wheat field rich brown, cut only a short time ago.

2014: Four lily plants in bloom today, only the naked lady with several blossoms.

2015: Michele writes: "Bill, We are hearing a bobwhite this morning over on Phillips Street. It has been at least 20 years since I have heard one!" Then Barbara Kerry left a message: she had heard a bobwhite, too, and even seen him (a male, she said) in her yard. "Last night a birding friend phoned to say she had heard a bobwhite calling up in tree between Whiteman and Davis Streets on Phillips. This morning I woke up at 8:00 to his call. My husband and I went down to the yard, and there he was walking around going toward High Street. I have not heard a male bobwhite since childhood, and I grew up in Miamisburg. It was just so awesome seeing him. Maybe we've got bobwhites back here again!"
    On further investigation, I found out that Mike Tripplet had let one of his caged bobwhites go a few days ago. Instead of a return of a lost species, the appearance of the bobwhite was a domestic, neighborhood fluke.

2016: Heat and dew, the yard so ragged, held together by zinnias and Mexican sunflowers, crabgrass and smartweed. A large-bodied orb-weaver set up in the dooryard garden over night, and I ran into one working near Jill's back porch last night. In the garden today, six cabbage whites at once, the most seen together this summer, one giant swallowtail, and a pair of male tigers working the circle garden zinnias and tithonias in the later afternoon. Climbing through the redbud trees, the bittersweet vines have berries that are fully formed but still green.

2017: Jill reported a monarch and a male tiger swallowtail. I saw the first red admiral butterfly of the year, oblivious to my approach as it explored pollen in the zinnias.

2018: First cardinal at 5:04 this morning. First katydid at 7:56 this evening. A small flock of geese, honking, flew over in the dark about 8:30.

So pure, so clear, so sweetly rare,
The answer steals upon the air—
Bob-White!

Marion Franklin Ham

August 12th
The 224th Day of the Year

In the season of late August star-fall,
When the first crickets crinkled the dark....

Robert Penn Warren

Sunrise/set: 5:43/7:36
Day's Length: 13 hours 53 minutes
Average High/Low: 84/63
Average Temperature: 74
Record High: 99 – 1900
Record Low: 46 – 1889

Weather

Today, the 13th and the 14th are usually sunny and dry, with a 15 percent chance of highs in the 90s, sixty percent chance of 80s, and 25 percent chance of 70s. Lows reach into the 50s half of the years, and into the 40s ten percent.

Natural Calendar

The Perseid meteor shower, bringing up to fifty shooting stars a minute out of the northeast, occurs after midnight between the 11th and the 14th. With the Perseids, the movement of birds south accelerates. Along the 40th Parallel, August star-fall also usually marks the end of the year's fireflies, the reddening of spicebush berries, the denting of the corn, the turning of soybeans, the commencement of the corn silage harvest, the last of the second cutting of alfalfa and the start of migration for male hummingbirds. Sumac horns are dark. Green acorns are coming down.

Daybook

1982: Got up to see the Perseid meteors at 4:00 a.m. Only three seen. Geese flew over the house just past dawn. I was restless all day, wanting to put things in place, walked out to Middle Prairie, took stock of what was there, what was changing.

1983: To Richmond, Virginia: From Yellow Springs through the mountains, the wildflowers remained stable: Queen Anne's lace, chicory, goldenrod, Joe Pye weed, sundrops, bull thistles, mustard, black-eyed Susans, wingstem, mullein, and sweet goldenrod. Hyssop (*Eupatorium hyssopifolium*) identified in bloom at the campsite.

1984: Williamsburg, Virginia: The jumpseed blooming stage here is the same as in Yellow Springs. Asters still not open here.

1985: On the way to Cedarville, I saw the first tall goldenrod turning. The first yellow jacket was at the fallen apples in the back yard. Tonight, katydids started singing at exactly 8:01 p.m.

1986: Geese fly over the house at 8:47 a.m. Color shift beginning in the tree line on the way to Wilberforce.

1989: Hummingbird moths still come to the impatiens. Dogbane pods at South Glen are up to ten inches long now, turning red. Last germander at Middle Prairie. Wood nettle mostly gone to seed. Lots of buckeye leaves are brown, many black walnut trees are weathering, yellowing. Patches of red in the sumac. Touch-me-not still full bloom. Tall nettle failing. Mint at the end of its cycle, teasel complete, tall bellflower still full, burdock full and late, wingstem early full and seven or eight feet tall, oxeye, tall coneflowers, early ironweed, late bouncing bets, fat patches of showy coneflowers, wild cucumbers full bloom, small flowered agrimony gone to seed, some poison ivy red. Cardinal singing almost exactly at sundown. Herons circling above the fog that is forming below me in the hollows.

1990: In the south garden, the late zinnias are finally opening. Mums are blooming. Showy coneflowers at their peak. Mallow almost gone. Yarrow weakening, tiger lily foliage is yellowing. Crickets sing in the morning now, maybe a new species recently born. My fall lettuce sprouted over night, winter zinnias and tomatoes for the greenhouse, too.

      At South Glen, most of the sycamore bark has fallen now. Japanese beetles continuing to mate, swarming on the sundrops.

Agrimony, tall bell flower, wingstem, Queen Anne's lace, ironweed, wild cucumber, showy coneflowers all flowering. Some bouncing bets are left, some old mint, wood nettle past its prime. Canadian thistledown, gray and matted, still hangs to its plants. Robins calling steadily, almost drowned out by the crickets and cicadas.

1993: I woke up at 4:00 this morning, listened to the katydids chanting. They stopped at about twenty minutes to five. No cardinals heard at all today, but they came steadily to the bird feeder.

1995: A cardinal sang just a little this morning, then he was quiet. Apples by the back door tree have almost all fallen. Crab apples turning at the park, some of the foliage tattered or eaten. The smell of the air has changed – it changed toward the end of July. August is the beginning of autumn like late winter is the beginning of spring. Like in late February and March, before any of the obvious signs have developed, I know winter is broken. Now by the first of August, I know summer is broken. The heat stays, but the rhythm has changed; all the tones have changed -- colors and sounds and scents all pointing to fall.

1997: Most of the resurrection lilies in the south garden are done by now, but they are in full bloom in the rest of Yellow Springs.

1998: Two-day vacation up to Lake Erie, bright large-flowered sow thistles all the way, purple ironweed, yellow wingstem, Queen Anne's lace common. No goldenrod open until we got close to the lake. Then, all across the northern edge of the state, the goldenrod remained blossoming. At the Crane Creek Park, the wetlands were full of purple loosestrife and the great pink water mallow. Complementing the loosestrife were the full heads of the blue vervain. Monkey flowers here and there, an occasional bouncing bet. In one backwater, dozens of giant, pale water lilies, probably the American lotus in full flower.

1999: This afternoon a dozen cabbage butterflies on the loosestrife.

2001: Screech owl heard at dusk, low whinny. Geese fly over silently after sunset. Katydids and crickets strident.

2005: Trees down all over town from yesterday's storm. Bob has a tree branch through his roof. Someone else, Dee said, had a branch come right into her bedroom. At the school, a large maple is down. Across from the church, the ground is covered with black walnuts. In the back yard, the first ironweed blossom opened in the middle of all the chaos of fallen trees. By the pond, the Royal Standard hosta came into bloom.

2008: Driving down through eastern Oregon and southern Idaho to the northern edge of the Great Salt Lake, across high desert that had been tamed with irrigation. The Snake River area is rich and surreal, vast plains against the distant backdrop of hazy mountains. Into Utah, the land becomes more intensely cultivated, many fields of corn tasselling. Very little prominent vegetation other than the omnipresent sagebrush, but some milkweed, wild lettuce, great mullein, a few sweet clover plants, one patch of loosestrife, and several other species not identified. I did hear crickets tonight – the first time I've heard them on this trip, and, really, the first time this summer anywhere.

    The real landmarks here are the mountains and the rocks; I want to know all their names, collect them like plants. As I drove, I wondered about the relationship of the people to the landscape, if they were overwhelmed by it, shaped by it, or if they retreated into the air-conditioned world of television and drugs of their urban and eastern counterparts. Either way, I was jealous of their access to such massive creatures and their naked geological history (like the giant dry lake near the Utah border). One would always have a point of reference, growing up beside a mountain. Is it the same with any aspect of home? Trees? Flowers? Birds?

2009: To Cincinnati: A Judas maple seen on the way to Byron. Some locust and cottonwoods yellowing throughout the trip. Ironweed in full bloom halfway to the Ohio River. False boneset opening at the zoo.

2010: Robins and cardinals at 5:00 this morning, continuing the summer chorus in spite of the rapidly lengthening night. Crows at 5:20, on schedule. A plateau of August birdsong and great numbers of butterflies day after day.

2012: Strong cardinals this morning at 5:15, robins in the background (the robins singing so deep into August – perhaps because of the early heat in spring and the warm summer. Did they have an extra brood?). Jumpseeds jumped when I stroked the plant that sticks out over the front sidewalk today.

2013: Madison, Wisconsin: Prominent prairie dock, cup plant, compass plant, Jerusalem artichokes, touch-me-nots, jumpseeds, goldenrod, purple loosestrife.

2014: Five lilies, four blossoms plus a cluster of naked ladies. The very first virgin's bower opened over night at Peggy's. Jumpseeds, fully developed and still soft, not jumping. A few orange lilies still in flower around town, scraggly. Walking in the garden this noon, I saw a spicebush butterfly, a painted lady (*Cynthia*) and a silver-spotted skipper all in one area of the north garden zinnias. Only a handful of fireflies tonight.

2016: Just three shooting stars seen with Jill at a little after 4:00 a.m. There have been no fireflies for over a week, so no false meteor sightings. In the yard, cabbage whites and occasional silver spotted skippers, male tiger swallowtails, and an Eastern Black swallowtail. On the road south, sundrops and purple ironweed in early full bloom.

2017: One polygonia (comma) at the koi pond this morning. A male tiger swallowtail sampling zinnia after zinnia this afternoon. An hour on the porch after dark: whistling crickets, high static crickets, katy-dids. The night was cool, no mosquitoes, no fireflies.

2018: Cool and sun: First cardinal at 5:03 this morning. Clusters of cabbage whites, four or more at a time. Golden fold-winged skippers playing, swooping in randori. Several monarchs, one giant swallowtail, one small Eastern black. Katydids started a little earlier this evening, at 7:51. A high-pitched cricket song began just a little earlier, a louder call, a whistling rattle.

There is still time. The colors and sounds of Late Summer promise everything.

Alonso Byrd

August 13th
The 225th Day of the Year

It is axiomatic that the same day never returns, that any act is done when it is done. It seems that at the end of August, summer is over. It seems that this summer cannot ever come again. Memory easily shows, however, that events do not end when they take place. Like the waves that form the Butterfly Effect, all happenings ripple time. And instead of receding from a present tense, this infinity of instances spins far out and then returns like a shower of shooting stars, shining children of comets, over and over again.

Leon Quel

Sunrise/set: 5:44/7:35
Day's Length: 13 hours 51 minutes
Average High/Low: 84/63
Average Temperature: 74
Record High: 98 – 1936
Record Low: 44 – 1964

Weather

Temperatures are in the 90s twenty-five percent of the days, in the 80s forty-five percent, in the 70s twenty percent, and in the 60s ten percent. Lows fall into the 50s forty percent of the nights, and into the 40s fifteen percent. Rain comes only one day in a decade, and skies are clear to mostly sunny nine days out of ten.

Natural Calendar

Once the mid-season hostas and the lilies are gone, Late Summer seems to pause. Under shooting-star-fall, defiant against encroaching autumn, the pastures, gardens and waysides show off Queen Anne's lace, trumpet creeper, horseweed, velvetleaf, wingstem, sundrops, blue vervain, small-flowered agrimony, tick trefoil, burdock, showy coneflower, ironweed, jimson weed, tall coneflower, ragweed, field thistle, boneset, clearweed, Japanese knotweed, willow herb, false boneset and rose pink. In the woods, leafcup, touch-me-not, tall bellflower, great blue lobelia, jumpseed, white snakeroot, Joe Pye weed and monkey flower are all in bloom. The green budding stalks of the tall goldenrod are poised, their full season still ahead, reassuring, promising the long-lived asters in another few weeks.

Daybook

1982: Walk along the railroad tracks and back through the woods: Queen Anne's lace, chicory, black-eyed Susans, burdock, wingstem, sundrops, trumpet creeper all still full bloom. Joe Pye weed growing old. One Asiatic dayflower seen. Flowering spurge and jumpseed first identified. Thimbleweed thimbles are prominent, avens mostly gone to burs. A few white scattered vervain and meadow goatsbeard.

1983: Richmond, Virginia to Manteo, North Carolina: Roadsides dominated almost exclusively by horseweed.

1985: The smaller maple in the yard has started to turn color, and is even losing a few leaves. One other Judas maple seen in town. Many catalpas are weathering, paling. Fireflies gone now.

1986: Butterflies everywhere this afternoon. Grackles cackling in the trees around the yard. This evening, I stood outside the back door and listened to the crickets dialoguing with the cicadas: first cricket chant, then cicada chant.

1988: First major morning fog. Japanese knotweed budding in the yard. Boneset still not blooming at the lower Grinnell Swamp. Spicebush berries still are green. Cardinal still singing off and on through the day. Doves and crows still prominent in the mornings. Cicadas begin by 8:00 a.m., continue for about twelve hours until the katydids take over just before 8:00 p.m..

1989: Wild cucumber, *Echinocystis lobata*, found in full bloom along the river in South Glen. A few fireflies left. Katydids began at 8:01 p.m.

1993: Doves still calling this morning. Balloon flowers holding on after I'd given up on them. Tall prairie dock on the corner of High and Limestone is in full bloom now.

1996: Lady slippers in the south garden have been past their prime for a week or so now, their pods breaking easily, shooting their seeds out onto the ground. Beside them, the tall pink asters have finally come into their own, are now in full bloom like tall bright mums.

1997: Fishing with John at Caesar Creek: Dozens of carp feeding in the shallows, much of their golden bodies visible above the water line. Great blue herons feeding with them. John caught a huge blue catfish late in the afternoon. It was rainy and cloudy most of the day; then when we were trying to get one more catfish at Cedar Hole, the wind shifted, and the cottonwood leaves started to rattle, the humidity fell, and the first breath of a cool front came across the lake.

1998: Headlands Park (along Lake Erie) to Yellow Springs: There are a few Judas maples along the lake. Cottonwoods are turning in the north, only a little ahead of home. Throughout the state, the season or trees and crops is still full Late Summer, the predominant color forest green. The landscape is covered with blue chicory, silver Queen Anne's lace, purple ironweed and field thistles, yellow wingstem and sow thistle.

1999: The hummingbird was back this morning a few minutes after 6:00. Phlox almost gone in the yard. Biennial gaura found in late bloom on the path north toward Springfield.

2001: First cardinal in the dark: 4:56 a.m., crickets still calling. Then blue jays at 5:23, crows at 5:25, crickets becoming silent. Boisterous bird song for maybe an hour, crows louder in the morning than I've heard them all summer. Then by 7:15, the sun well up over the horizon, the excitement tapers off. The rest of the day belongs to cicadas.

2002: An old black swallowtail, wings tattered, was resting in the west garden this afternoon, allowed me to come right up to it. Several other swallowtails visited the yard today looking for zinnias. Only two fireflies seen tonight.

2005: Whistling crickets when I got up this morning at 4:55. Sing-song crickets came in at 5:10, cardinals at 5:15, dove by 5:20, robin peeping at 5:25 – and a three-noted call, hollow, almost ghostly, but like a bell call, too. Geese at 5:55. A family of six chickadees hunted for insects in the old apple tree at 3:00 p.m.

2008: Great Salt Lake to Laramie, Wyoming: Jeanie and I followed I-80 along the Overland Trail, through the deep gorge and pass leading into Wyoming out onto the broad, flat land of the high plain across the southern part of the state. Vegetation remained simple: sage brush, a little sweet clover in wetter areas, and three very common wildflowers – the yellow-flowered knapweed-like plant I photographed in the badlands, and two other plants I have little hope of identifying on this trip.

2009: More black walnuts on the ground. Peak of purple morning glories in the alley. One great ragweed plant loaded with golden pollen. A tiger swallowtail visited the butterfly bush all day.

2010: More swallowtails and monarchs today. Only one firefly seen tonight. Prairie dock full bloom at the corner of High and West South College streets.

2011: Returning to Yellow Springs, the day filled with cicadas in the trees, monarch butterflies, cabbage whites (and three in mating randori), hummingbird moths, silver spotted skippers and smaller bi-fold winged skippers, a small golden crescent, a buckeye, a great spangled fritillary and a zebra swallowtail. The humidity here feels friendly and accepting - Portland was so dry and aloof. The grass is ready to cut after a week away, and the weeds have come back to fill all the spaces that were clean on August 5th. In the garden, zinnias, butterfly bushes, heliopsis, Joe Pye weed, early ironweed, an early mum plant, some gooseneck, the pale pink giant hibiscus, two resurrection lilies and knockout roses give color to the yard. Hidden under the rusting crabapple tree, the first white blooms of the Royal Standard hosta promise a rich August and September. Cicadas and katydids at 8:00 p.m.

2012: Robins and cardinals still sing before dawn. Very few butterflies today. This evening, only field crickets at 7:00, then tree crickets by 7:15, katydids by 8:00.

2014: The August 10 – 12 cold front settles in, chilled by the full moon and perigee. In the garden, four lily plants hold on. A painted lady (*Cynthia*) butterfly visited the zinnias about 8:30 this morning, a male tiger and a tattered spicebush and a monarch this afternoon.

2015: Portland and Beaverton, Oregon: Rudbeckia, reblooming lilies, Shasta daisies common. Many pink spirea bushes with a few pink blossoms left, tattered rose bushes. A simple and subdued urban habitat of Deep to Late Summer.

2016: Muggy, warm, thunderstorms and sun: Cardinal at 5:09 this morning. Doves heard after sunrise. As I watched for about half an hour around noon: three male tiger swallowtails, numerous silver-spotted skippers, two fritillaries, a hummingbird and several finches in the circle garden tithonias and zinnias.

2017: Many cabbage whites, a few fold-wing skippers, one silver spotted skipper seen through the day. Then one monarch came to the zinnias at 5:00 p.m. after I had been waiting an hour in the back yard talking to my sister Tat.

2018: Almost all the phlox are gone now, knotweed has sent out its budded fingers, and the first jumpseed seed jumped when I stroked it. Monarch butterflies in the garden throughout the day, and one Eastern black, one giant swallowtail, one male tiger swallowtail seen.

Thus shall ye think of all this fleeting world
A star at dawn, a bubble in a stream,
A flash of lightning in a summer cloud,
A flickering lamp, a phantom, and a dream.

The Diamond Sutra

August 14th
The 226th Day of the Year

Live in each season as it passes; breathe the air, drink the drink, taste the fruit, and resign yourself to the influences of each.... In August live on berries.... Be blown by all the winds.... Grow green with spring, yellow and ripe with autumn. Drink of each season's influence as a vial, a true panacea of all remedies mixed for your special use.

Henry David Thoreau

Sunrise/set: 5:45/7:33
Day's Length: 13 hours 48 minutes
Average High/Low: 84/63
Average Temperature: 73
Record High: 95 – 1965
Record Low: 44 – 1964

Weather

Chances of highs in the 90s are 15 percent, for 80s fifty-five percent, for 70s thirty percent. Rain falls two years in ten on this date, and the sun almost always shines. Chances of lows in the cool 50s are 40 percent.

Natural Calendar

High Katydid Season marks the slow decline of Dog Day Season this week of the year. Migration seasons intensify for wood ducks, Baltimore orioles and purple martins. This is the week of Cottonwood Foliage Yellowing Season and Joe Pye Seeding Season, the time of Three-Seeded Mercury Season and Great Blue Lobelia Season. It is the week during which Spiderweb Weaving Season becomes more noticeable throughout the woods, spiders taking all the prey they can before cold settles in. Firefly Season moves to a close as Late Summer Monarch Butterfly and Swallowtail Butterfly and Imperial Moth Seasons swell. As Apple

Windfall Season pulls windfall apples to the earth, Autumn Yellow Jacket Season reaches into the Northeast.

Daybook

1984: At Coquina Beach, Outer Banks, North Carolina.: Many plants at similar stages to those in Yellow Springs: red berries on the pokeweed; wild lettuce, ragweed, horseweed, bindweed, primrose, smartweed in full bloom. Other species identified which I have not found in Ohio: marsh mallow, sea oats, white-top sedge, horsemint, maritime ground cherry, buttonweed, trailing wild bean, beach evening primrose, pennywort all in bloom.

1985: No cardinals before dawn for days now.

1986: Cardinals woke me up at 5:10 this morning; they continued off an on until around noon. Geese flew over at 8:30 a.m., and I heard them again faintly in the evening. Three-seeded mercury blooming in the garden.

1992: The garden holds steady after the lilies are gone. Phlox, zinnias, cosmos, coreopsis, showy coneflowers, purple coneflowers, an occasional balloon flower, snapdragons, mums growing up around them. The flicker still sings in the back trees, but cardinals have been quiet for about a week.

1996: Ever since the 8th, the weather has been cool. The fogs these past two mornings have been heavy, the air wet and cold, the dews thick. The cottonwoods seem to turn more each day. Fall appears to be here already, this Late Summer too prophetic, too dramatic. First monarch seen in the garden today.

1997: Fishing with John along the river: Two carp and a mud turtle caught on night crawlers. At home, the purple loosestrife completes its cycle in the pond and in the north garden. The last resurrection lily fades here, still strong in the village.

1998: Jeanie cut back the purple loosestrife in the pond today, all but a few fragments of flowers gone (the opposite of its full bloom along Lake Erie). Wren eggs discovered in the pitcher plant on the front porch.

1999: One resurrection lily finally bloomed in the south garden, but throughout town, they have been in full bloom for a while. The frog is quiet in this cool wet day, insects hiding. Cardinals at 5:15 a.m. Hummingbird at 6:15 a.m.

2000: August hostas are in full bloom here and throughout town. Two cutover spiderworts blossoming in the south garden. Arrowhead full in the pond, water plantain gone for a while now, collapsed by the side of the fountain. Some fallen leaves along the bike trail. Dry leaves from the front maple were lying on the sidewalk and the street this morning. Praying mantis found in the garden yesterday. Barbara Preis's mantis has come back this year again, the third or fourth year at least. So it's possible that the mantis I came across was a descendent of the mantis I found there some years ago.

2001: At 4:50 a.m., only crickets. At 4:56 a.m. one cardinal, then silence until 5:14 when cardinals called throughout the neighborhood for about 15 minutes, but just off and on. At 5:21 a blue jay, 5:25 a few crows, then silence. A wren at 5:45, a few crows in the distance at 6:10, then it was daylight and quiet.

2004: At Saugatuck in Michigan: Two days of clear skies and cool winds. The habitat here still shows orange day lilies and turban lilies, making it about two weeks behind Yellow Springs. Purple loosestrife lines the highways, thick and rich. Ladybugs seemed to be migrating along the beach, getting caught in the low waves and the sticky sand. Cardinal flower, boneset, heal all, St. John's wort, white campion, purple vetch, wild mint (*Menta arvensis*), hawkweed, late hoary alyssum *(Berteroa incana)*, horse mint, soapwort, knapweed, Canadian goldenrod found. Arrow wood viburnum, its berries dark purple, identified at a northern rest area. Only a few butterflies. Five deer seen in the woods of pine, spruce, ash, red oak.

2005: Spicebush swallowtails and monarchs come to the garden every day. Sometimes tiger swallowtails and giant swallowtails, too.

2008: Laramie, Wyoming to Gothenburg, Nebraska: We left the high desert of Wyoming and, crossing the state line at Pine Bluff (which is actually full of pines and bluffs), entered the greener fields of Nebraska, even great corn fields that seem to have flourished without irrigation. The vistas of Wyoming remained, only greener and maybe even wider. The rock and cliff formations disappeared, and the roadside flowers gradually become more numerous, starting with sagebrush and gumweed and then adding some sweet clovers – yellow, white and purple, banks of common sunflowers and many other plants not identified. At the campsite in Gothenburg, a rich habitat that included tall three-seeded mercury, catnip, a thin-leafed germander, salsify, a rough-leafed ragweed with sharp, pointed leaves, a great Indian plantain type of plant, purple grapes on the wild grapevines, many dark berries still hanging to a red mulberry tree, white sweet clover and others. Upon our arrival this afternoon, Jeanie heard hundreds of cicadas – for the first time since we left Ohio. And at night, crickets!

2009: Walking Bella at 8:30 a.m. No doves heard, a few cardinals in the distance. A squirrel whining in the Limestone Street trees. Privet berries getting big. Moya's white-flowered hostas in full bloom, and the violet-flowered hosta in the east dooryard garden. Rapidly fading purple coneflowers. Full bloom of winterberry vines in the back trees. Tiger swallowtail, giant swallowtail, and a monarch seen throughout the day.

2010: No birdsong at 5:00, but full chorus plus crows at 5:20. Swallowtails at the butterfly bush again today. Resurrection lilies have been gone for several days. One crab apple at the park is losing berries. One fallen peach at home. Faint robin vespers at 6:30 this evening. This afternoon, Jonatha wrote: "I have exclaimed all summer at the number and variety of butterflies. I do not remember so many since my teens, back in Missouri. As a child I loved them all, learned their names, took specimens and photographs." Jonatha also sent notes by Nancy Stranahan dated

August 12 of this year: "You see, this is the year. A year not only for berries, but also for butterflies, too. We might not experience a summer like this again in southern Ohio for another ten years."

2011: 4:00 a.m.: Full moon setting behind the locust trees, after a soft, long night rain, low broken, round clouds from due west allowing the moonlight in creases and lumps. High-pitched screech of tree or ground crickets, very clear. Another level, lower, of that type of cricket, katydids weak and distant. I stand in the dark, blind to the sources of the sounds, aware that I can only hear a fraction of what is happening around me. But my hearing aids allow me to have a sort of revived puberty of hearing, an awakening of that sense. The first cardinal sings at 5:07 a.m. (I ruminate more about the fragments that I perceive, about how incompletion is the normal state of things, how immersed I am but isolated too, separated from the exterior world by my inability to actually sense what is holding me in place.) Steady cardinal calls and high crickets continue. Color appears in the zinnias by 5:30. Crows awake at 5:35. Cardinals quieting down a few minutes later. (I conclude that perfection of being in this place must accept all the immensity of my inability. All the nature I do not find with my senses must have to come from the acceptance of limits, from accepting and allowing freely the myopia that I bring to observation, the coming to terms in myopia, taking in the single, separate, so incomplete, events: the necessity and consolation of synecdoche.)

2012: Cardinals began at 5:14 this morning, robins joining a few minutes later.

2013: Madison, Wisconsin: Cardinals sing occasionally through the day. Only a few cabbage white butterflies seen today. Walking through the park near Maggie's house, the paths blocked by great stands of tall coneflowers and touch-me-nots, at the same stage, it seems, as in Yellow Springs. Identified pink flowering *Polygonum amplex* in Tat's garden, full bloom.

2014: The best day yet for butterfly sightings: Two spicebush swallowtails and a black in the Glen, and at home a monarch, a male tiger swallowtail, a great spangled fritillary, a painted lady (*Cynthia*), and numerous cabbage whites and skippers. Along the wooded path to the Yellow Spring in North Glen, the very first goldenrod was opening, a shorter variety than in the fields. All the usual flowers blooming: wood nettle, touch-me-nots (yellow and orange), leafcup, wingstem, jumpseed, early black snakeroot. All around the yard and in the Glen, clearweed (*Pilea pumila*) is in full bloom.

2016: Cardinal heard outside my window: 5:35 this morning. Rain throughout the day as a huge band of storms stalls across the eastern half of the country, but gradual cooling takes place as the August 10th front inches toward Pennsylvania. Throughout the village, the coneflowers are conspicuous. Leafcup lines the woods along the bike path, scattered wingstem here and there. The plantings of the Women's Park have lost their freshness. Milkweed pods are full size. Record flooding reported in Louisiana.

2017: One large yellow sulphur and one male tiger swallowtail, many cabbage whites and skippers in the garden this afternoon. The resurrection lilies in town have wilted and fallen over.

2018: Monarchs and swallowtails continue to visit the garden throughout the day. Maggie sent photos of her nine monarch caterpillars.

Above the arching jimson-weeds flare twos
And twos of sallow-yellow butterflies,
Like blooms of lorn primroses blowing loose,
When autumn winds arise.

James Whitcomb Riley

August 15th
The 227th Day of the Year

Nature has, for the most part, lost her delicate tints in August. She is tanned, hirsute, freckled, like one long exposed to the sun. Her touch is strong and vivid. Mass and intensity take the place of delicacy and furtiveness. The spirit of Nature has grown bold and aggressive; it is rank and course; she flaunts her weeds in our faces. She wears a thistle on her bosom.

John Burroughs

Sunrise/set: 5:46/7:32
Day's Length: 13 hours 46 minutes
Average High/Low: 84/63
Average Temperature: 73
Record High: 98 – 1965
Record Low: 45 – 1964

Weather

The Midwest continues to be dominated by high pressure – which can linger for up to a week after its arrival near the 10th. (Sometimes the stagnation of that weather system can bring tropical-like conditions.) The likelihood of highs in the 90s is relatively low - just 20 percent. Temperatures in the 80s are common; they occur 55 percent of the time, and mild 70s come 30 percent of the days. Cool nights in the 50s continue to be recorded four years in ten, and the chances of rain begin to rise, climbing from yesterday's 15 percent up to 25 percent. The likelihood of completely overcast conditions also increases to 25 percent.

The Weather in the Week Ahead

The weather in the third week of August is somewhat stable, bringing highs in the 90s on 15 to 20 percent of the afternoons, milder 80s fifty-five percent of the time, and cool 70s the remaining 25 percent. The 19th of the month, however, breaks from the pattern many years, and it has the highest frequency of 90s (35 percent chance) of any other day in the week. Chances of rain increase from 25 percent at the beginning of the period to 30 percent by August 21st, then drop abruptly to just 15 percent on the 22nd.

Natural Calendar

Rows of gaunt great mulleins, black and gone to seed, line the bike paths and roadways. Pokeweed plants are the size of small trees, with purple stalks and berries. The panicled dogwood shows pale fruit, its leaves fading pink. Staghorns darken autumn brown above their red or yellow leaves.

But goldenrod brightens the fields, and the height of Tall Bellflower Season softens the mood of the decaying forest undergrowth with blossoms of powder blue. Beneath them fat, white puffball mushrooms emerge like moons among spring's rotting stems and leaves.

Daybook

1983: Walking along the shore of Manteo, North Carolina, the beach of the Inland Waterway: Wild lettuce and bindweed, both with leathery leaves, in bloom here. Mullein, rough-leafed burdock, wild grapes are still green, pokeweed at the same stage as in Ohio.

1985: Goldenrod slowly turning. Ash, maples, catalpas, cottonwood yellowing from the heat and drought. A few dogwoods are violet red. The gray-white flowers of the false boneset dominate the roadsides to Xenia.

1986: A cardinal wakes me up at 5:20 a.m. Geese fly over at 9:27 a.m., and then at 7:05 p.m. At the upper Grinnell path in late afternoon, the last flowers of the season are getting set to open. Bur marigolds are budding, also zigzag goldenrod, broad-leafed swamp goldenrod, and small-flowered asters. A few dark berries on the spicebush. Water horehound and swamp milkweed still open, still a few tall bellflowers, a little wood mint. Jumpseeds aren't jumping yet. Patches of gold on the Osage and cottonwoods, one maple yellow green, poison ivy red. Cardinal singing throughout my walk.

1987: First frost in the country reported: 28 degrees in Montana this morning.

1988: Cicadas suddenly become quiet when a thunderstorm passes just north of town. At Ellis Pond, the blue vervain is at its peak, first goldenrod budding, peak of the summer's fireflies this evening (their season set back weeks by the drought).

1989: A quiet day: only an occasional dove call. No crows, blackbirds, sparrows, cardinals, wrens, blue jays.

1990: Snow in northern Canada reported, as the first of the autumn air masses moves down into the northern states. Warm in Yellow Springs, the height of golden wingstem, purple ironweed.

1993: Four fall-red raspberries yesterday, another four today, three of the second crop of strawberries: the late seasons starting. White phlox declining now in the north garden, disappear over night in the south garden. Some zinnias just coming into bloom. Two or three balloon flower buds left. Mulberry leaves turning along the south hedge. The fruit has been gone probably since the end of July – along with most of the grackles. Honking geese fly over the west end of town at 7:03 p.m. A few minutes later, half a "vee," silent over the house.

1996: I noticed that the very first leaves on the front yard maple have turned just a little, the progress of the past few days. In the rose garden, Japanese beetles making a comeback, maybe a new generation born. Geese flew over today, and yesterday, their flights becoming more frequent. In a field beside Wilberforce-Clifton Road this morning, a flock of geese was feeding in the alfalfa.

1998: Cardinals sing at 5:25 a.m., crows call at 5:35, blue jays at 6:43.

2001: First cardinal this morning 5:12. Doves and crows at 5:24. Scattered birdsong until about 5:45, then silence. Squirrel chattering at 5:38. No blue jay heard. One yellow jacket seen, not in an apple as usual but in the body of a dead mouse one of the cats had brought home. No other yellow jackets seen so far.

2002: Short-tailed ichneumon found in the greenhouse.

2005: Resurrection lilies continue full bloom throughout the village.

2006: In Portland, Oregon, the foliage and flower sequence seems to be about the same as it is in Yellow Springs, patches of yellow on cottonwoods and maples, chicory and Queen Anne's lace common by the roadsides, roses full bloom, late Japanese honeysuckle, pumpkins ripening.

2007: Portland, Oregon: Raspberries done, blackberries at early full fruiting. Jeni's everbearing strawberries are sweet, abundant.

2008: From Gothenburg, Nebraska to near Des Moines, Iowa: The greening of the landscape intensified as we drove east. Sunflowers disappeared for a time, then reappeared, stronger and taller from the increase in rainfall. Chicory reappeared for the first time since we left Minnesota two weeks ago, then bright purple ironweed, yellow primroses, Queen Anne's lace, goldenrod (full bloom and just beginning), gray coneflowers and other coneflower varieties, field thistles, partridge pea (at the campsite), tall nettle, tall mullein, great ragweed, an unidentified white medium-sized field flower, probably false boneset. The increasing variety of roadside flowers was matched by the deepening of the richness of color in crops and grasses. In Iowa, the corn and beans were so lush that some of the plantings even appeared blue in the distance. We had passed from the western dry high plains to the fertile Heartland farmland.

2009: Frank's lilies hold. Tall coneflowers full. Apple tree with some leaves browning. One black swallowtail, a monarch and the same tiger swallowtail that has been here for several days. I thought about the interplay of season lengths, the simultaneous passage of shorter phases within the ongoing passage of longer phases. Within the broad range of summer, all of the summer flower seasons rise and fall; those floral spaces create patterns within which other patterns and plateaus occur.

2010: A bright yellow male finch was feeding four fledglings at the thistle feeder this afternoon. Along the roads, the bottom leaves of corn are finally turning brown.

2011: A monarch and several tiger swallowtails today.

2012: First cardinal at 5:14 this morning, robinsong a couple of minutes later. Faint patches of color in the roadside trees, blushing of a few leaves here and there, black walnuts, maples, box elders. Two spicebush swallowtails, one hummingbird moth today, vespers from the doves at Ellis Pond at sundown.

2014: Bright, cool day once again. Two naked lady clumps and two small, yellow reblooming lilies in flower. Along North High Street, the purple coneflowers are fading (as they were yesterday somewhat at the Women's Park). The white autumn alliums at the corner of Dayton and High are fully budded. Two monarchs in the Joe Pye flowers and one great spangled fritillary, a very bright yellow and orange sulphur, and a male tiger swallowtail in the zinnias, as well as numerous folded-wing skippers, silver-spotted skippers throughout the flowers this afternoon. Phlox and Joe Pye blossoms, along with the zinnias, still keep banks of color all along the north garden.

2016: Steady rains have bent all the tall, red amaranth stalks, and one patch of zinnias has collapsed in upon itself. The Shasta daisies are down to their last blossoms, and the heliopsis is cluttered with brown, stained blooms. Throughout the garden, it is time to cut back spent flowers. Yesterday evening and then in the night, a new, loud, rattling call that must be from a kind of frog.

2017: Leaving Yellow Springs in fog: the prairie dock at High and South West College streets was early bloom, maybe half a dozen blossoms. To western New York state: Queen Anne's lace, chicory, Joe Pye weed, fringed loosestrife, ironweed, goldenrod (the shorter variety in full bloom, the taller just opening), white-flowered teasel, and drifts of Japanese knotweed and wild cucumber in flower. When we stopped at a roadside parking area away from the highway and the rush of trucks and cars, I felt a relief in the quiet, surrounded by soft grasses speckled with thin-leafed buttercups, two daisies with separated, floppy petals, purple heal all, white clovers, a few hawkweeds and dandelions. This was such a plain and ordinary habitat, its sparse vegetation a simple and finite mandala, unplanted and undesigned that, for some reason, separated me from the complexities and risks of the long pre-autumn trip, some vague sadness which I must have caught from the gray and lumpy cumulus and stratus clouds, and the rank Johnson grass and prickly teasel of the rougher and wilder freeway borders.

2018: This afternoon; A great spangled fritillary, monarchs (three at one time), cabbage whites, a silver spotted skipper. Looking back over the Late Summer and Early Fall daybooks, I get a sense of the tide shifting, the Great Change coming in. The story quickens and deepens.

In fields
along old trails, at pasture edge,
the ironweed bares its vivid tint,
profoundest violet, a note
from farthest star and deepest time,
the glow of sacred royalty
and timbre of eternity....

Robert Morgan

August 16th
The 228th Day of the Year

O, greenly and fair in the lands of the sun,
The vines of the gourd and the rich melon run..

John Greenleaf Whittier

Sunrise/set: 5:47/7:31
Day's Length: 13 hours 44 minutes
Average High/Low: 84/63
Average Temperature: 73
Record High: 98 – 1965
Record Low: 47 – 1963

Weather

This date brings a 30 percent chance of highs in the cool 70s, a 55 percent chance of 80s, and a 15 percent chance of 90s. Chances of a shower as well as for totally cloudy skies are 30 percent. Nights in the 40s come one year in ten, 50s three in ten.

Natural Calendar

As the Sun moves toward its halfway point to equinox, frost season opens in the Northwest, and snow will soon be falling into Hudson Bay. Elderberries are ready for wine throughout the country.

Daybook

1982: To Wisconsin: Goldenrod seen in western Ohio and again in northern Indiana. Maples are turning in Madison, Queen Anne's lace, chicory, spurge, white snakeroot, burdock, great mullein, black-eyed Susans, sundrops, Joe Pye weed, trumpet creepers all blooming close to Yellow Springs levels. Motherwort flowers are shriveled and prickly like at home. Heavy goldenrod bloom on the way north to Marshfield.

1983: Cape Hatteras and Okrakoke Island: Ragweed and pokeweed common and at the same stage as in Yellow Springs. Yarrow still in bloom, but fading. Lamb's quarters, remnants of pepper plants, small-leafed purslane, and water hemlock are open, thin-leafed tick trefoil in bloom, and meadow beauty, white-top sedge, small-flowered partridge pea, some goldenrod, sea pink, too.

1986: Goldenrod just barely turning along Grinnell Road.

1990: Katydids begin at 7:57 p.m., a little earlier than last week, the sun setting a little earlier.

1999: The hummingbird comes to the rose of Sharon again at 6:15 a.m.

2000: One black walnut tree on the way to Fairborn completely bare.

2001: Cardinals two minutes late this morning, sing at 5:22 a.m. Doves follow at 5:24, crows at 5:27. Jay at 5:38. Squirrel at 5:45. The neighborhood quieting by 6:00, silent by 7:00.

2003: Portland, Oregon: Resurrection lilies seen in full bloom on the way to the airport. Returning to Yellow Springs after a week out west: A cottonwood tree along the freeway is half turned. At home, Joe Pye and phlox are still in bloom. Ironweed has opened. Zinnias and dahlias have replaced almost all the day lilies. Royal Standard hostas are blossoming; they were just budding on the 9th when we left for Oregon.

2004: Tussock moth caterpillars are eating Greg's butterfly weed.

2007: Return from Portland. Some turning of the trees there, perhaps because of drought. Yellow coneflowers, a variety of the *rudbeckia speciosa* in full bloom throughout Portland. Most phlox gone now here at home; yellow coneflowers have become the dominant planting, make Yellow Springs and Portland seem to be at the same point in the year. This morning, it was quiet at 5:00 a.m. Robins began to chirp at about 5:10, cardinals at 5:20, then all the calls stopped at 5:40. A new brood of cabbage butterflies seen at the purple speedwell – at least nine at one time. Monarchs and tiger swallowtails at the zinnias and tithonia throughout the day.

2008: From Iowa down to Moraine View State Park near Bloomington, Illinois: Small flock of starlings seen along the route – the first so far this Late Summer. The land continues bright and lush, the corn tall and strong, the soybeans unbelievably green. Queen Anne's lace dominates the roadsides as sunflowers and clovers disappear. Ironweed is relatively common throughout, as are some gray-headed coneflowers, goldenrod and probably wingstem. Field thistles are both budded and blooming. Now that we are back along the 40th Parallel and have come down from the high plains, Yellow Springs time controls the landscape. And – if anything appeared clear throughout all this trip - it is the broad applicability of the Yellow Springs world to the entire nation.

2009: Again the tiger swallowtail that has frequented our butterfly bushes floated down from the high white mulberry tree this morning and began working the purple blossoms. In the alley, a few of Mrs. Timberlake's orange lilies still flower. The black walnut tree behind Jerry and Lee's house is turning and shedding. A bat found dead in the lawn this afternoon. An August hosta transplanted to under the east apple tree.

2010: Robins around 5:00, crows raucous at 5:23 until about 5:30, occasional calls for another ten minutes. Robin singsong lasting throughout much of the morning. The butterflies came early today, tiger swallowtails, spicebush, fritillaries, monarchs. At noon, there were three spicebush, a tiger swallowtail, a monarch and a fritillary in the flowers. Driving in the countryside, we saw four monarchs.

2011: No robins for weeks, it seems, but cardinals still sing around 5:15, and crows came through this morning at 5:35, exactly the same time as yesterday morning. Three male tiger swallowtails on the butterfly bush this morning, the most at one time so far this year. One common buckeye came by also, a sign of Late Summer in Ohio, as the buckeyes migrate north, crossing the Ohio River in August. Yellow leaves spotting the birch tree near the park, and one black walnut tree on Fairfield Road. Sparrow fledglings still begging for food through the afternoon. On my walk tonight with

Bella, field crickets were the most common sound (near 7:00 p.m.) for the first time, the tree crickets holding back (then exploding with the katydids after dusk. First orb-weaver spider seen tonight by the front window.

2012: Robins singing from 5:08 - maybe a little earlier - this morning. Few cardinals until after sunrise. One tiger and two spicebush swallowtails seen at random today. Two Judas maples seen on the way to and from Beavercreek. Phlox down to maybe a fourth of their blossoms. Some people have reported Joe Pye flowers gone to seed. Lynn brought a small bag of peaches from her trees, said they had been coming in for maybe a week. Our first windfall peach is almost ready to eat.

2013: Inventory at home after a few days in Madison, Wisconsin: Lily patches all overgrown, but naked ladies/resurrection lilies still flower. Dahlias, butterfly bushes, Shasta daisies, the tall red and the tall pink hibiscus, Royal Standard and other August hostas, Joe Pye, late phlox, very late spiderwort, re-bloom of Indomitable Spirit hydrangea and some Knock-out roses offer most of the perennial color. Heliopsis and monarda almost completely gone. Peaches late this year, still hard, maybe three-quarters developed. Butterflies: one monarch (the first of the year here in the yard), a spicebush, Eastern Black, a male tiger swallowtail, numerous silver-spotted skippers and cabbage whites. Moya's August hostas are in full bloom, and Peggy's virgin's bower has its first flowers.

2014: At the Monastery of St. Clare near Cincinnati: The woods mostly bare of any flowering plants, but the edge of the property contained smartweed with white, wavy stems, a lush clump of horse nettle with white flowers, and several lanky, very elegant plants, very much like upland boneset (*Eupatorium sessillifolium*) but with longer leaf stems than shown in my references (therefore not "sessile" or clasping). And also flower stems in the bracts. This afternoon at home I heard an exquisite robin valediction, a long warbling song that seemed to bring together so much emotion about the passing summer.

2016: A cardinal woke me up at 5:30 this morning, both of us sleeping late. More precipitation throughout the day. This afternoon, I cut back one patch of zinnias that had toppled from the rain, cut all but four of the Shasta daisies. Now the heliopsis flowers are almost completely gone, and the zinnias that held up through the storms need to be clipped to encourage more blossoms. One male tiger and a hummingbird in the tithonias today in spite of the rain.

2017: One Judas maple seen near Keuka Lake in New York, one Virginia creeper with red-purple edges on some of its leaves. Fog low across the lake at sunrise, lasted several hours.

*Old wortermelon time
is a-comin' round again.*

James Whitcomb Riley

August 17th
The 229th Day of the Year

The humming bee fans off a shower of gold
From the mullein's long rod as it sways,
and dry grow the leaves which protecting infold
the ears of the well-ripened maize.

William W. Fosdick

Sunrise/set: 5:48/7:29
Day's Length: 13 hours 41 minutes
Average High/Low: 83/63
Average Temperature: 73
Record High: 98 – 1908
Record Low: 43 – 1902

Weather

Today is the last day that temperatures above 100 are likely to occur for the rest of the summer (although the slight possibility remains through the first week of October). Almost three-fourths of the afternoons, however, are in the 80s, the remaining fourth in the 70s. The sun appears 70 percent of the time, and showers pass through four days in ten. Evening lows are in the 60s seventy-five percent of the nights; they fall to the 50s fifteen percent, to the 40s ten percent.

Natural Calendar

Plums and pears are ripe in the orchards, and the summer apple harvest is more than half complete along the 40th Parallel. Farmers are making preparations for the seeding of winter rye, wheat and barley. Second-brood corn borers, the second generation of bean leaf beetles and the rootworm beetles still feed in the fields. Banded ash clearwings attack local ash trees.

The Stars

In the night sky, the Summer Triangle shifts into the west, following June's Corona Borealis and Hercules. Delphinus, the

Dolphin, is due south. After midnight, autumn's Pleiades rise up over the northeastern tree line. Orion fills the east before dawn.

Daybook

1983: Manteo, North Carolina: Poison hemlock in full bloom here, and early great mullein, too – actually behind Yellow Springs. Heat, rainfall, wind, soil conditions, and cutting patterns have all combined to equalize the summer seasons.

1985: A huge flock of geese flew over the house at 7:40 p.m.

1989: The panicled dogwood near the stream on King Street has its first white berries.

1987: The tropical storm season is underway in the Caribbean, first storm named a week ago. In central Indiana, catalpas, poplars, cottonwoods have faded and some are yellowing, soybeans a third turned, some corn browning, late thistles full bloom.

1989: A quiet day: only an occasional dove call. No crows, blackbirds, sparrows, cardinals, wrens, blue jays heard.

1991: Northern Minnesota near Crookston: Most commercial sunflowers are done blooming, but some patches are still bright, faces still up. White sweet clover is still open here, even a few parsnips (early June in southwestern Ohio). Several varieties of goldenrod wide open.

1992: Resurrection lilies still full bloom in town. On the bike path south, tall mulleins, black like dead cacti, all the way to Jacoby.

1993: On Stafford Street, a blush of red to a small redbud tree. At Mills Lawn, one black walnut has thinned to maybe half its leaves, some of its fruit fallen. A cluster of yellow black walnut leaves has come down on High Street just a few feet from our yard. In the north garden this afternoon, a flurry of black walnut leaves came down into the asparagus bed from the tree on other side of the hedgerow. At Wilberforce, many crab apple leaves destroyed by skeletonizers, some trees almost bare. Still an occasional firefly in the back yard.

1997: A few fireflies tonight in the warm, wet evening. Thunderstorms moving across the valley.

1998: No fireflies seen for so long; the drought of the past month deepens. Cardinals sing at 5:25 a.m., crows about 5:40. Flocks of geese flying over Yellow Springs the past two days.

1999: Fishing today at Caesar Creek: Buzzards overhead and great blue herons every few hundred yards. A family of ducks came begging for food at my boat, then moved on. The tree line is yellowing: cottonwoods, box elders, ashes, maples. Coneflowers and ironweed, Joe Pye weed, swamp milkweed still in bloom. Wild grapes are dark purple. One catfish caught today and yesterday, pan fish biting at the pan fish hole. In the countryside, some cornfields stressed and withered by the drought; others are completely brown and dead. At the dairy, a baby bird, all pink, an inch long, had fallen from its nest to the picnic table.

2001: The waning moon rising over Glen Helen at 4:50 this morning; above it was giant Venus, a little further up, Jupiter. The Pleiades led them on. Only crickets called until 5:12, then a faint song from a cardinal. At 5:26, crows, 5:28 a blue jay. At the school park, two black walnut trees are almost bare. Along the freeway, one cottonwood has lost most of its leaves. At South Glen, the first jumpseeds were loose, just able to jump.

2003: Whistling crickets when I got up at 4:30 a.m., fourth quarter moon high in the southern sky. At 5:00, no birds. Cardinals heard at 5:30, then silence. Crows continue to stay away from Yellow Springs, but several people I've talked to recently say crows are still common where they live in other suburbs. One monarch noticed today, several tiger swallowtails.

2004: One arrowhead flower appeared in the pond today, but the plants themselves are not strong this year, are deteriorating along with the rest of the pond vegetation.

2005: Two painted lady (*Cynthia*) butterflies in the zinnias late this afternoon. Monarchs and swallowtails common throughout the day. One arrowhead plant is in full bloom in the pond.

2007: Stonecrop sedum starting to flower in the east garden.

2008: Moraine View State Park in Illinois to Yellow Springs: Two monarchs and a relatively large flock of starlings seen on the way home, vegetation all quite typical: sundrops, horseweed, field thistles, sometimes miles of blue chicory, Queen Anne's lace, ironweed, hawkweed, wingstem.

2009: Cardinals and doves still singing from about 5:15 on this morning. Crows passed through an hour later. Two days ago, I saw a swarm of small ants crossing the sidewalk along Dayton Street. This morning as I walked Bella at about 9:15, I saw another mass movement of similar-size ants. Two flocks of starlings seen in Beavercreek and Dayton. The first pink stonecrop flowers opened in the east garden this afternoon.

2010: Robins at 5:10 this morning, cardinals at 5:20, crows late at 5:30. No doves heard for at least a week. Several monarchs, red admirals, tiger swallowtails and spicebush swallowtails in the butterfly bush at lunchtime. Four hummingbird moths sipped nectar at the same time.

2011: Cardinals again this morning, 5:09 a.m. One dove heard when I walked Bella after breakfast. Only a couple of orange day lilies bloomed today; they are reaching the very end. Some of the rebloomers keep on coming in, however. Sparrow fledglings still begging. Five cabbage butterflies on the catmint this afternoon. Screaming cicadas tonight at 7:00 p.m. and occasional field crickets.

2012: Overcast morning, cold front still off to the east in Indiana, no cardinals or robins until 5:30. Some of the stonecrop in the dooryard has been in flower for well over a week. First large bowl of peaches for breakfast this morning: full peach time has begun. Resurrection lilies have disappeared, heat stressing the zinnias, phlox and Shasta daisies ebbing.

2013: Only field crickets chirping and tree crickets buzzing heard when I went out at 4:40 this morning. First cardinal heard at 5:24, no robin calls before or after dawn. Tiger swallowtails, hummingbird moths and hummingbirds seen here and in Cincinnati, starlings on the power lines along Dayton-Yellow Springs Road, robins beginning to flock in the woods by the St. Clare monastery. An ochre tint to some of the cottonwoods, a shadow of pale gold through some of the soybean fields.

2014: Cardinals throughout the neighborhood this morning singing at 5:14, sky clear, half moon overhead, bats passing above me, constant, loud static of crickets. Crows and doves at 5:45. Only two lilies blooming – the fading naked ladies. Four male tiger swallowtails (one quite old and tattered), a giant swallowtail, and several silver-spotted skippers, cabbage butterflies and folded-wing skippers worked the zinnias while I made notes outside on the porch and then hauled wood. In our pond, arrowhead has passed its best, some leaves yellowing, most flowers to seed. At Ellis yesterday, a small mint (*Menthe arvensis*), has spread in the grass, in full bloom by the side of the pond. I will try it in with the arrowhead at home.

2015: Return from Oregon: The amaranth plumes have kept their color, even though the stalks have grown too tall and are falling over. The heliopsis is ragged and mostly rusted (and full of red aphids), and I cut back a lot of it – along with mats of monarda and rusted tall ferns. (The heliopsis, the zinnias, the amaranth, the hydrangeas and the monarda should all be supported with open fencing or strings next year.) The huge red hibiscus flowers have all wilted on the main stalk, a couple left on a side stalk. The tithonias have pushed out all the zinnias – but have filled in several holes left by the drooping hydrangeas and spent lilies (overgrown now by smartweed). The Joe Pye flowers have begun to decay as the goldenrod buds become more prominent. Jeanie's stunted yellow rose has one flower – the first of the year. The first purple ironweed in the yard came into bloom, nestled among the tithonias. Japanese knotweed is in full bloom – I hadn't noticed it before I left a week ago, and the wisteria that has taken over the trellis has several flower clusters – like the wisteria next door to Jeni in Portland, Oregon. Moya's white moonflowers are all open, and in Peggy's garden, early virgin's bower and the white autumn allium are in bloom. A few swallowtails and a monarch seen around home today.

2016: So much like last year. The purple ironweed even started to bloom over night. One male tiger swallowtail, and the first sulphur I've seen all summer.

Nature does not cast pearls before swine. There is just as much beauty visible to us in the landscape as we are prepared to appreciate, - not a grain more.

Henry David Thoreau

August 18th
The 230th Day of the Year

The field of Nature being beyond the power of any one man to cultivate in full, let everyone begin with his own parish, and till that area intensively.
Gilbert White

Sunrise/set: 5:49/7:28
Day's Length: 13 hours 39 minutes
Average High/Low: 83/63
Average Temperature: 73
Record High: 97 – 1895
Record Low: 48 – 1899

Weather
Chances of highs in the 90s are 15 percent today; they are 60 percent for 80s, and 25 percent for 70s. Rain comes four times in a decade on this date; completely overcast conditions occur as frequently. Evenings cool to the 40s or 50s one night in five.

Natural Calendar
The third week of August brings Judas Maple Time to the Lower Midwest. Complementing that maple season, Sumac, Poison Ivy and Virginia Creeper Reddening Seasons grow along the fencerows. In the woodlots, Wild Plum Season compounds the sweetness of Elderberry Season. Whip-Poor-Will, Cedar Waxwing and Catbird Migration Seasons open. Goldenrod Season presages September as Ironweed Season and Wingstem Season continue to brighten the landscape.

Daybook
1985: Railroad tracks north: Wild grapes are purple now. Plums sweet and ready for jelly. Virgin's bower full bloom, and willow herb, both the yellow and the blue-flowered wild lettuce, thin-leafed coneflower, tall nettle, oxeye, prickly mallow, small woodland sunflower, soft velvetleaf, sundrops, heal all. Elms and poison ivy turning pale yellow. Great blue lobelia found. Clusters

of cabbage butterflies and monarchs. Most mulberries here are gone. Greenbriar with blue-black berries. At home, the bull thistle plant came into bloom.

1986: No cardinals heard today. Long flock of blackbirds or grackles crossed Mad River heading north.

1990: Cicadas, crickets, katydids still at their peak. Cardinals quiet in the morning, a pattern of silence now.

1993: Mother finch still feeding her baby in the cherry tree this morning.

1997: Crows this morning instead of cardinals. The sky is gray, the air heavy with old summer, foliage all around the yard becoming a darker, duskier green. Along the back roads, more and more weathering of the leaves, more shading.

1998: Cardinal sings at 5:25 a.m. Crows call at 5:30.

1999: The hummingbird came to the pond at 5:59 this morning, hovered for a minute eating insects. Ten minutes later she was back sipping nectar from the rose of Sharon.

2000: Virgin's bower, Japanese knotweed and jumpseeds are all in bloom, a full range of white patterns both low and high. At the corner of Limestone and Stafford streets, I saw a Judas maple, the first noticed this year; then, paying attention, I found Judas ashes and Judas walnuts almost every block. Fog was hanging across the fields as the evening cooled.

2001: First local goldenrod barely starting to show color. First jumpseed jumps.

2002: Tiger swallowtails have been coming to the garden all through August. This morning, one more, then a giant swallowtail, then a spicebush swallowtail, several cabbage whites, and an orange skipperling. In the south garden, phlox are done, but many patches in town are still strong. Showy coneflowers are still at their best. Some second bloom on the monarda. The hydrangea has finished flowering in the east garden.

2004: A large camelback cricket in the bathtub this morning. It sat in my hand as I brought it out to the greenhouse. All the tomatoes picked yesterday – pasta making today. The seasonal tide is turning so quickly now, the cool summer intensifying and becoming the feeling of fall. So many trees with touches of color.

2005: Stopped briefly at South Glen: Wild cucumbers, tall coneflowers, leafcup, yellow touch-me-nots, white snakeroot and jumpseed were in full bloom. Burs on the burdock, ready to stick. Red leaves on the path from Virginia creeper throughout the trail. Tall bellflowers were on their last blossoms. Wood nettle was declining, a few leaves turning white. Brittle, black seeds of the sweet Cicely scattered when I fingered their clusters. Linden and oak at the triangle park are turning. In the garden, new clusters of cabbage butterflies flutter around the Joe Pye weed.

2007: Robins at 5:13 a.m., one cardinal at 5:33, a dove about five minutes later. Then all the birds are quiet by 5:45. Joe Pye weed has rusted, and coneflowers, Queen Anne's lace, Shasta daisies, and the remaining heliopsis dominate the garden. Annuals and white-flowered Royal Standard hostas provide plenty of life in the shade. Webworms noticed in Janet's redbud.

2008: Return from a three-week trip west to find the garden in pretty good shape. A monarch butterfly came to the orange Mexican sunflowers as I reviewed the flowers: Heliopsis and Shasta daisies, giant, deep red hibiscus, Joe Pye weed, rose of Sharon, late purple coneflowers, very late mallow, some larkspur and speedwell, full showy coneflowers, Endless Summer hydrangeas, white, purple and red phlox, budding false boneset. Fingerlings are still alive in the pond, the frog still lurking. Cherries have disappeared from Don's tree. A giant swallowtail in the new zinnias this morning, and a cardinal sang at 5:15 and a little later, too – then quiet. Lots of cabbage butterflies in the garden through the day. Arrow-shaped *micrathena* spiders common now in the wooded parts of the yard. In Florida, Tropical Storm Fay moves through the Keys and the Gulf side of the state.

2009: The hurricane season starting late, Hurricane Anna fizzled out over Cuba and Hurricane Bill is heading up into the North Atlantic. Here, one monarch seen at Moya's. Great ragweed still heavy with golden pollen in the alley. Cardinals began at 5:22 this morning, sang for maybe three-quarters of an hour. Squirrel whining at 6:10. Two tiger swallowtails and what seems like a new hatch of cabbage butterflies in the butterfly bush this afternoon. More lettuce planted this evening. I also put in a row of beets and a few cabbage plants I found by the side of the street the other night.

2010: Robins around 5:00 this morning, cardinals at 5:10. Three tiger swallowtails in the butterfly bush this morning at 10:15, an Eastern black, a spicebush, an orange sulphur, and a monarch at noon. More hummingbird moths. Sparrow fledglings being fed. Katydids begin singing at 7:50 p.m.

2011: Cardinals called from about 5:15 this morning for about twenty minutes, then quiet for a while, hummingbirds moving in on the feeders, then the sparrow flock arrived, the rhythm of their leader about fifty-five chirps a minute, a little slower than I found in Middle Summer. Squirrel chatter more common now since we returned from Oregon. No robins for a long time, disappearing a month ago as the rains stopped and heat in the 90s lasted day after day. Two monarchs, one spicebush, one tiger, one rare red-spotted purple swallowtail seen today. Webworms seen along Fairfield Road, but really very little webworm webs seen this Late Summer. Our river birch and cherry show early turning. The black walnut tree by St. Paul's church has lost half its leaves.

2012: Cardinals and robins heard at 5:15 this morning. One tiger swallowtail, one spicebush. A large flock of starlings swooped back and forth across the sky as we drove east toward Cedarville this afternoon. In much of eastern Greene County, the corn and soybeans are stunted or withered. On the road to Cincinnati: old teasel and field thistles, banks of horseweed, many trees bare - stressed from drought and heat. In Wilberforce, the locusts where I used to park are still green. At home, Tim's black walnut is almost bare; the walnut by the church is shedding but has kept most of its leaves so far. Peggy's virgin's bower is fully budded. Liz's Joe Pye weed and some of ours are going to seed. A buckeye butterfly in the zinnias by the bedroom window near midday. No birdsong vespers tonight.

2013: More yellow tiger swallowtails, four or five in the garden now, and silver-spotted skippers and more cabbage whites.

2014: Doves still call in the morning. One male tiger swallowtail when I was outside this morning. Cicadas and static crickets very loud. Another tiger and a giant swallowtail in the afternoon. Black walnut foliage yellowing along Corry Street, one reddening maple by the college. At the mill habitat, full Late Summer: glades of bright wingstem, patches of tall bellflowers, scattered ironweed, huge heal-alls, boneset, touch-me-nots – yellow and orange.

2015: A cardinal calling when I was up at 5:30. Three monarchs seen throughout the day in the zinnias and giant tithonias. I noticed that the pokeweed berries had started to turn purple while I was gone last week.

2016: The first fog of the Late Summer this morning, the grass so long and wet. One male tiger swallowtail seen visiting the garden this afternoon. In a corner of the north garden, behind the knotweed, the first pokeweed berries have turned purple. Ruby's daughter, Jane, reported a reddening leaf.

2017: Walking along Bluff Road on Keuka Lake in New York, we saw orange jewelweed, trefoil, boneset, sweet peas.

I used to sit on the Spring Slough Trestle to read and write and dream, spending time as wisely as I knew, watching the years pass, at first slowly, and then with increasing swiftness, and never counted a moment there ill spent.

August Derleth

August 19th
The 231st Day of the Year

Summer's robe grows
Dusky, and like an oft-dyed garment shows.

John Donne

Sunrise/set: 5:50/7:26
Day's Length: 13 hours 36 minutes
Average High/Low: 83/62
Average Temperature: 73
Record High: 102 – 1936
Record Low: 51 – 1964

Weather

The 19th is often the warmest day in the third week of August, bringing highs in the 90s on 30 percent of all the years. Temperatures reach the 80s forty-five percent of the time, stay in the milder 70s the remaining 25 percent. Nighttime lows are in the 60s eighty percent of the time, and chances of rain continue at yesterday's 40 percent.

Natural Calendar

Cicadas chant from an hour or so past sunrise to dusk. The crickets start in about half past seven in the evening. By eight o'clock the katydids have joined them, replacing the cicadas, and chanting *katydid* until morning when sometimes there is a brief period of silence, and then everything starts all over again.

Daybook

1986: No cardinals heard today. As I was driving to Springfield, I saw a long flock of blackbirds heading north. Fishing at Sycamore Hole: carp or chubs stole bait for an hour, then left, return, biting and thieving again in two hours.

1989: Leaves turning a little now in patches across the far tree line. Coneflowers in the south garden continue full, as does the mallow.

The second crop of raspberries, light for the past three years, is coming in slowly. I picked a handful about the 15th, another today.

1990: Tomatoes ripening all at once, and zucchinis begin to flower again. Mosquitoes return with the rain. A few fireflies.

1992: To Kalamazoo, Michigan: Goldenrod starts to bloom just past the Michigan border.

1993: Into South Glen: Wild cucumber common climbing through the wingstem, and purple ironweed is at its best. Across Middle Prairie, a tint of gold from the small locusts. At Mills Lawn Park, a yellow poplar has started to turn.

1999: At four this morning, the crickets were loud, no katydids. Then at about 4:15, one or two katydids started in, called for a few minutes, then silence. Now at 5:52 a.m. no bird sound yet, the sky dark.

2001: A cool and cloudy morning, crickets singing: the cardinals didn't start until 5:31. Six minutes later, the first dove, followed almost immediately by crows. Then a cardinal flew to the apple tree, first motion of the day. Faint, intermittent bird calls through sunrise. Even though so many apples have fallen, no yellow jackets have come to find them this year.

2002: No birds at 4:20 a.m., faint cardinal song at 5:00 then fairly common from 5:20 on. First mother-in-law tongue blooms on its long stalk.

2003: Virgin's bower seen in bloom along Walnut Street.

2004: Very few butterflies have come to the garden this month, no monarchs since the end of July. The pink stonecrop in the east garden is starting to open now, and the Japanese knotweed along the street is in full bloom.

2005: Cardinals at 5:25 a.m., faintly in the distance, a gentle crescendo of volume for maybe 15 minutes. Doves at 5:35.

2006: Inventory on returning from Portland, Oregon: Resurrection lilies still in bloom, and white phlox, Shasta daisies, rose of Sharon, Royal Standard hostas, black-eyed Susans, July-planted gladiolas, cut-over Heliopsis, roses, ironweed, Queen Anne's lace, violet mallow late. Joe Pye graying, virgin's bower budding. Web worms in the white mulberry and Janet's redbud. Peaches still hard but sweet. Through the countryside, banks of bright chicory, sundrops and Queen Anne's lace, corn still green with golden tassels, soybeans deep forest green fields stretching for miles, milkweed pods prominent by the roadsides, apples red. On the way to Goshen, Indiana, nine small flocks of starlings seen, one medium flock of blackbirds or grackles. One snout-nosed butterfly seen on the back deck. In the alley, tall coneflowers have completed their season, thin-leafed coneflowers now in full bloom, goldenrod blushing.

2007: Robins started to sing at 5:20 this morning, and a cardinal called at about 5:30. Complete quiet at 5:40 until the crows arrived at 6:30 and called until 7:30. Through the alley, the tall coneflowers and the thin-leafed coneflowers are fully flowered. Blue bindweed covers one of the east fences. Mateo's goldenrod is turning, but the other goldenrod is still just blushing. His black walnut tree has shed about a third of its leaves. The black walnut by the Catholic church hasn't really lost much.

2008: Cardinal at 5:30 this morning, strong until about 6:00. In the alley, the tall coneflowers are in full bloom. Mateo's black walnut is yellowing and starting to shed. The apples look ripe on the apple tree, some fruit starting to fall. Burdock full bloom. The last two lily buds in Mrs. Timberlake's yard are set to open today or tomorrow. Some feverfew left, too. Great ragweed still holds its pollen. Moya's white-flowered hostas fill her yard. I saw Doug Hinkley downtown about 10:00; he said he had seen a flock of several hundred grackles flying into the southwest. In the yard this afternoon, nine white cabbage butterflies, a late brood hatching, and Jerusalem artichokes in the south garden covered with dark aphids (a late-summer hatching – like the butterflies?). Chiggers were waiting for me; my legs are itching.

2009: Humid, cloudy morning, rain off and on. Doves but no cardinals heard this morning. Scorpion fly seen hunting in the bean vines.

2010: Robins singing at 5:00, cardinals at 5:20. No crows heard until after sunrise. Swallowtails (tiger, spicebush), monarchs, skippers and hummingbird moths continue to visit the butterfly bushes. One last orange day lily opening. No stonecrop flowers in our yard yet (but open at the artisans' store). Our new red myrtle is in full bloom, and the first flowers have appeared on Peggy's virgin's bower. Three fireflies seen last night near Moya's house.

2011: More squirrel chatter today. A dozen-plus cabbage whites playing in the yard all day. One monarch, one spicebush, one tiger swallowtail. Thunderous katydids and crickets tonight.

2012: No birds heard this morning until cardinals sang at 5:25. Crows at the west end of the village at 5:35, robins not coming in until well after 6:00. Late hostas continue to come into bloom, phlox and Shasta daisies almost gone. Crepe myrtles in full bloom along the north wall and in Xenia.

2013: Heavy fog early morning, gossamer webs everywhere, wet and bright. Three yellow tiger swallowtails at the butterfly bushes and zinnias this morning, and more skippers, cabbage whites, hummingbird moths. Resurrection lilies are fading everywhere in town, and most of the gladioli have finished here and at Lawson Place. Crepe myrtles not blooming yet. Webworms cut from Jeanie's redbud and from the volunteer red mulberry by the bedroom window. Four tiger swallowtails came by while I was eating supper on the porch. A sluggish scorpion fly landed on my shirt, reluctant to fly when I brushed him off. From Annie's window this evening, I saw a few fireflies signaling.

2014: No robins heard or seen. Cardinals, however, continue before dawn: 5:19 this morning, with doves in full song by 5:40. Four lily plants still struggle to produce their last flowers. Moya's August hostas: drifts of white blossoms, my late hostas open, too.

At night screaming whistling crickets, intense static from trigs; Peggy seems to have all the field crickets. Katydids throughout.

2015: Cardinals still singing in the morning. Webworm webs seen near the highway south. Not a single lily today, their foliage yellowing and rusting. Through the day: occasional monarchs, Eastern blacks, a female tiger swallowtail, blues, golden skippers, silver-spotted skippers, cabbage whites. Sudden loss of color in the Joe Pye weed. No hummingbird moths seen since the monarda season ended.

2016: The first cardinal sang in the back yard at 5:31. Another morning of fog. From an hour or so outside: one monarch sighting, one giant swallowtail today, one small black swallowtail, one great spangled fritillary, one brown. And a catbird in the old mock orange, the first I've seen here in years. A few Stella d'oro blossoms struggle in the overgrown east garden by the gate. Jill's thin-leaved coneflowers continue to provide a strong drift of color near her driveway and back entrance. In the pond, the koi are ravenous and swim rapidly back and forth, frolicking throughout the day. At the Catholic graveyard, many green acorns from a white oak near the roadway.

2017: Returning from Keuka Lake in western New York, I noticed a number of maples turning, and the rest of the forests deep August green. At home, the Royal Standard hostas have bloomed under the crab apple tree and across the street. In the late afternoon, Jill saw a monarch in her garden.

2018: At the Glass Farm wetlands in the cool morning, very thin fog, August overgrowth throughout, spreading up to the vegetable gardens of the people living up the hill, great ragweed and horseweed in bloom and foxtail grass nodding, occasional sundrop primroses and chicory. A monarch landed in front of us as we walked, and another came by when I got home to the zinnia garden. And then I saw that the old peach tree had fallen over night, blocking the path. The original tree still stands behind it, long dead. The grandchild of that tree is just a little taller than I am. In the water willows toward the pond, a few web worm webs –

and one small one in the flowers at the back of Jill's yard. At the triangle park, one crab apple tree is full of red leaves, and at home, the hackberry has thinned to maybe half its foliage. Tonight no cardinal vespers, but the crickets were screaming. The katydids started to rub their legs together at 7:45 sharp: "katy-katy-katy-did did-did-katydid-katydid."

That summer I began to see, however dimly, that one of my ambitions, perhaps my governing ambition, was to belong fully to this place, to belong as the thrushes and the herons and the muskrats belonged, to be altogether at home here. It is a spiritual ambition, like goodness. The wild creatures belong to the place by nature, but a man can belong to it only by understanding and by virtue.

                        Wendell Berry

August 20th
The 232nd Day of the Year

This is the time when elms wear most profoundly
Their air of revery,
Drooping over the tarnished slopes of Late Summer.

Clara Shanafelt

Sunrise/set: 5:51/7:25
Day's Length: 13 hours 34 minutes
Average High/Low: 83/62
Average Temperature: 73
Record High: 98 – 1983
Record Low: 50 – 1897

Weather

Today is typically warm and humid, partly to mostly sunny, with rain four years in ten. Distribution of high temperatures: 20 percent 90s, forty percent 80s, forty percent 70s. Early morning lows find 40 three years out of ten, reach into the 50s five years in ten. Odds for a day in the 90s are only half of what they were two weeks ago, and the likelihood of highs in the 70s is twice as great as it was at the end of July.

Natural Calendar

Beggarticks unfold their small golden flowers at this stage of Late Summer, coming into bloom as Judas maples become more common. Hickory nuts lie on the woodland paths. Buckeyes are completely formed. The panicled dogwood foliage reddens a little, its berries green. Acorns are full size, a few even a rusty brown.

Purple pokeweed berries shine through the undergrowth. Burrs of the tick trefoil catch on your pants legs. White vervain is gone, and the flowers of blue vervain climb to the top of their spikes, measuring the end of warmest time of year. Fields of brilliant oxeye, coneflower, goldenrod, wingstem and ironweed hide the decay of Canadian thistles, fringed loosestrife, skullcap, wild petunias and meadow rue.

Phlox and resurrection lilies and gladiolus flowers disappear quickly. Golden showy coneflowers have begun their three-week process of decay, and the menacing ragweed is becoming old and empty. Along highways, the umbels of Queen Anne's lace, so bright through Middle Summer, are contracting and darkening.

Telephone wires fill with birds as migrations accelerate. Flickers, redheaded woodpeckers, red-winged blackbirds, house wrens, scarlet tanagers, Eastern bluebirds, robins, grackles and black ducks move south. Bees work harder. Spiders weave more webs. Grackles and starlings become louder in the afternoons, but an entire morning can go by without a cardinal song or the sound of a dove.

Daybook

1982: First goldenrod flowers seen in the county.

1983: Hops seen in bloom. First maple leaves in the yard are turning.

1984: Chincoteague Island, Maryland: Marsh mallow, partridge pea, swamp rose mallow, meadow beauty, fog fruit, salt marsh fleabane, horseweed, salsify, pennywort, common ragweed, goosefoot, pokeweed, smartweed, dayflowers, sea pinks, horse mint, St. Andrew's cross, water parsnip, swamp milkweed all in bloom.

1985: Buckeyes are completely formed now, their shells smooth, cream colored. New basal leaves noticed on the sweet rocket, probably appeared several weeks ago; next year has begun.

1988: Swamp beggarticks just budding at upper Grinnell, white snakeroot still fresh, starlings thick in the evening trees.

1989: On both sides of the South Glen paths, walls of golden wingstem and purple ironweed.

1990: Cardinal sings once at dawn, then is quiet.

1991: All across southern Michigan a fuchsia tint lies on so many shrubs and trees.

1998: First yellow jacket noticed in the fallen apples. One pale spicebush swallowtail, all its color faded, wings tattered, visited the garden.

2000: Yellow jackets and large black and white hornets all over the fallen apples this cool sunny afternoon. A few black walnuts came down over night onto High Street.

2001: Cloudy, rainy morning. Cardinals at 5:33, crows at 5:37, jay at 5:41, wren-like chatter at 5:53. I didn't hear the doves join in at all today.

2002: One Eastern black swallowtail seen today, one yellow tiger swallowtail, one monarch. Purple coneflowers are gone at the Women's Park, the showy coneflowers fading there, too. Water plantain full bloom in the pond.

2004: Fall webworms found in one redbud and the white mulberry, the first all summer. Virgin's bower is blooming in Hustead, just north of Yellow Springs, and another vine is starting near here on Elm Street.

2005: Sitting on the back porch late this evening, I watched fireflies blinking in the yard, one every few seconds.

2006: Fireflies disappeared this year in July.

2008: Two fireflies seen in Tony's field last night. A cardinal sang at 5:30 again this morning, continued for a while. Cabbage butterflies abundant today. August Moon hostas are opening along the south border of the yard. Light leaf fall of crab apple trees at the triangle park. The ash tree at the southeast corner of our property has started to yellow. Honeysuckle berries are reddening. Several maples are turning pale. One apple tree almost bare at the entrance to town. Euonymus vines are in full bloom along the west border of the yard.

2009: I woke up at four this morning, listened to the katydids chanting. I had been reading Anthony Storr's *Solitude*, and I lay in bed thinking about his note on the perception of order: "The human mind seems to be so constructed that the discovery, or perception of order or unity in the external world is mirrored, transferred, and experienced as if it were a discovery of a new order and balance in the inner world of the psyche."

And so I took inventory of the external world here through the day. At South Glen, dogbane pods are up to ten inches long now, turning red. Wood nettle blossoms still strong, holding late this year. Soft drifts of touch-me-nots full bloom. Tall nettle still fierce but failing. Mint at the end of its cycle, teasel complete, tall bellflowers still climbing their stalks, burdock getting burs, wingstem, oxeye, tall coneflowers, fat patches of showy coneflowers, wild cucumber vines full of white blossoms, small flowered agrimony gone to seed, early ironweed with purple-blue flowers on stalks six feet tall.

So many buckeye leaves are brown, black walnut foliage weathering, falling Most of the sycamore bark has come down now. Patches of bright scarlet in the sumac. A shower of yellow hackberry leaves from just one side of a branch. One cardinal singing almost exactly at sundown. Two blue herons circling above the fog which formed below me in the hollows. Robins calling steadily, almost drowned out by the crickets and cicadas.

I think that what can happen in noting such details is that a kind of order is experienced (whether that order reflects some actual pattern or not), and once that unity is internalized, then there is a breakdown of alienation, a personalization of an otherwise indifferent context.

Then seasonal time and place fill the eye of the beholder, producing an act of possession that is a step toward self-hood and then of making sense and of finding home in which nothing is out of place. Recognizing what is here: always discovery.

2010: Spicebush, Eastern black and tiger swallowtails all day today. At noon, the Eastern blacks whirled around and around in an intense randori. Throughout town, many black walnut trees have thinned to maybe half their leaves. In the back yard, we found one more tent caterpillar tent, this one in the white mulberry, just out of reach. The very first pink stonecrop buds have opened in the dooryard. Jeni saw two fireflies when she walked Bella tonight.

2011: One tiger swallowtail, one long green, striped caterpillar with a green horn on its tail, didn't fit any of the pictures I could access. On this morning's walk: high-trilling crickets, cicadas, field crickets, and a red-tailed hawk circling the village, crying out, "creeee."

2012: Faint robin song at 5:20 this morning, but no cardinals heard until after sunup. Wren chattering near dawn. "Handsome trig" found on the car later in the morning, may be the kind of insect that makes the high static cricket sound at night. One sparrow fledgling seen being fed. Bright finches still come to the feeders.

2013: More yellow tiger swallowtails and another giant swallowtail. The very first sedum flowers in the dooryard opened over night.

2014: Cardinals at 5:24 this morning, crows at 5:37, doves by 5:40, no robins. A bright, warm day with numerous cabbage whites, silver-spotted skippers, several male tiger swallowtails, a giant swallowtail and an Eastern black. One naked lady and one rebloomer the only lilies still open.

2015: An inch of rain in a storm yesterday evening pulled over most of the amaranth, Joe Pye and tithonias: August – cutting down time. But in the faded Asiatic and Oriental lily bed, one small white stargazer that Jeanie had planted was blooming this morning, the very last lily of the year. This afternoon, I walked into the orb-weaver web across the shed door. How many years have I done that!

2016: Dove heard before 5:30 this morning. To Cincinnati in heavy fog: sundrops, and dominant horseweed, late darkening Queen Anne's lace, wild cucumber wandering through hedges, brown teasel, rows of glowing (but not flowering) goldenrod, a few naked ladies, one treetop covered with a webworm web (the first noticed this August). I came home in light, intermittent rain to a monarch butterfly hanging out in the zinnias. Last night, Rick told me he had seen glowworms glowing in the grass and monarchs visiting his flowers.

2017: In the sunny zinnias: one red admiral, two small silver-spotted skippers mating, occasional cabbage whites. Took milkweed to Barbara Carroll to feed her monarch caterpillars she had captured from her garden. Working in her back yard, Jill saw a monarch, her second since our return from New York. In my northwest garden, the Joe Pye weed is all gray, and the heliopsis is three-fourths finished. My Royal Standard hostas are now in full flower, and Moya's August Moon hostas fill her yard with white blossoms. In front of Don's house on Dayton Street, his thin-leafed hostas are starting to put out violet flowers. My thin-leafed hostas have budded stalks but no flowers.

2018: A white Stargazer lily that Jeanie had chosen, one of the last to survive the weeds of the past several years, opened yesterday evening. This morning in the sun, two monarchs played together all around the zinnias.

In the long rays of the last light of that mild August evening, I looked and saw that the chlorophyll had begun to drain from the long stems of the water plants, that a line of brown had begun to form at the waterline of the pond. I noticed that with the sun suddenly down, the air had become unexpectedly cool against my bare arms.

Paul Gruchow

August 21st
The 233rd Day of the Year

Yet a few sunny days in which the bee
Shall murmur by the hedge that skirts the way,
The cricket chirp upon the russet lea,
And men delight to linger in thy ray.

William Cullen Bryant

Sunrise/set: 5:52/7:24
Day's Length: 13 hours 32 minutes
Average High/Low: 83/62
Average Temperature: 72
Record High: 100 – 1936
Record Low: 46 – 1950

Weather

Showers come three years out of ten today, highs in the 90s ten percent of the time, 80s six years in a decade, 30 percent for a day in the 70s. Skies are clear to partly cloudy 70 percent of the time. Lows in 60s occur on 80 percent of the nights, cool 50s on the remaining 20 percent.

Natural Calendar
An Incomplete Chronology of Leafturn during Early and Middle Fall in a Typical Yellow Springs Year

August 10: Black walnut trees have started to shed. Leaves often begin to yellow on cottonwoods, locusts, box elders, spicebush and crabapples.

August 20: Orange patches have appeared on a few Judas maples. Many locusts are brown from leaf miners. Buckeyes can be half yellow. The earliest ash trees blush.

August 30: Some catalpa and black walnut trees have lost most of their leaves.

September 5: Cottonwoods fade more dramatically as goldenrod and the soybean fields turn gold.

September 10: Silver olive foliage has streaks of ocher.

September 20: Ashes start their autumn transformation, some becoming maroon, others gold. (After the die-off of the early 21st century, ash-turn is no longer a marker for autumn in many locations.)

September 25: Black walnut trees are completely bare. Crab apples and hackberries are thinning. Color spreads across the red maples. Blush appears on the sweet gums. Box elders are shedding.

October 1: Enough leaves have fallen from the canopy to reveal the deep red of the Virginia creeper on branches and fences. Amber hickories blend with the ashes. White birch leaves show gilded edges.

October 5: Enough orange maples, yellow sumacs, hickories, redbuds and red oaks have now joined the ashes and cottonwoods to give a full sense of autumn to the landscape. The burning bush is deep scarlet. Beeches are flushed for their November change. The late fields of goldenrod, the dry corn, and the rusting soybeans complete the fall scenario.

October 10: Peak leafturn is starting to occur in woodlots where maples, ashes, buckeyes, wild cherry and locusts predominate. Most Osage are yellow now, a few ginkgoes starting. Cottonwoods and the rest of the box elders lose their leaves, and more holes open in the tree line. Fencerows are shedding their Virginia creeper. Grape vines hold on yellow-green.

October 15: Witch hazel, the last of the flowering shrubs, opens. Rains often take down the ashes and redbuds by this date, ending Early Fall. Full Middle Fall begins, bringing in the remaining maples for approximately a week.

October 20: White oaks are crimson, and the end of soybean harvest and the browning of goldenrod finally subdue the glowing September fields.

October 25: Silver maples are champagne gold, and the sugar and red maples are down or are shedding quickly. Tulip trees are almost gone. Some ginkgoes are green, others fully gold and losing foliage. Light frosts accelerate the passage of Middle Fall.

October 30: Osage, sweet gum, ginkgo, and white mulberry continue to keep their leaves. Beeches are half turned. Maples collapse in storms. Some sycamores are totally undone; others are only thinning as the mottled land enters Late Fall.

November 5: The pear trees are red brown. Sweet gums are coming down. Ginkgoes and white mulberries reach their brightest, and then disintegrate.

November 10: Rose of Sharon shrubs are half bare. Honeysuckles weaken, berries becoming more prominent. Across the countryside, the woodlots are dark and empty.

Daybook

1984: Snow reported in Hudson Bay. Lows in the 40s now common across the northern states.

1988: Swamp beggarticks and zigzag goldenrod are just budding at upper Grinnell. White snakeroot still not full bloom. Starlings thick in the evening trees.

1991: Flicker calls 6:55 a.m., long quarter-of-an-hour song, then silence. No cardinals or doves heard in the morning, one dove called in the afternoon. Mill Habitat: Love vine full bloom. First goldenrod flowering, most of it ready. Still high Late Summer, the peak of the blue lobelias and the jumpseed (not jumping), coneflowers still full, and wingstem and ironweed. Insects still everywhere. Tree color holding.

1992: At Caesar Creek: sun, 70s, light wind, waning moon. A Judas maple here and there, some red Virginia creeper leaves, but the tree line basically uniform. Only the vaguest color has begun, the faintest yellowing. Smell of wood smoke in the air. The first hurricane of the season (Andrew) reported in the Caribbean heads northwest toward San Juan (will eventually devastate much of southern Florida). At my second fishing hole, the poison ivy is red along the bank. Honeysuckle leaves becoming a little pale. Cicadas still strong. Paniceled dogwood reddens a little, berries green, spicebush with a hint of violet, love vine leaves are orange, hops full bloom, hanging dense down over the water. Willows seem dry, rusted. Water horehound full bloom on the stump habitats, leaves purple, mad dog skullcap found there too, *scutellaria lateriflora*. Biennial gaura identified along the bank. Monkey flower very late, beginning to decay. Common arrowhead late bloom. Joe Pye still bright and strong, trumpet creeper holding. Blue vervain middle to late full bloom. Boneset holds, sundrops, Queen Anne's lace, great ragweed. The water quiet, but large schools of minnows near the surface. No birdsong most of the day. One blue heron flew silently upriver. One robin peeped. Maggie called from Madison, Wisconsin: Jack-in-the pulpit berries had just turned red there. Bergamot is fading, she said. Purple coneflowers almost gone, peak of goldenrod.

1998: Cardinal sings at 5:27 a.m., crows a little later, blue jay at 6:02.

2000: First cardinal at 5:31 a.m. Crows moving in by 5:45. Sundog in the west this afternoon, maybe an hour before sunset.

2002: One Aphrodite fritillary at the zinnias this afternoon. One tattered yellow tiger swallowtail in the grass. Two more monarchs in the north garden. At eight this evening, two bard owls talking back and forth at South Glen: "Who cooks for you?" Flowers found in bloom: jewelweed, wood nettle, tall bellflower, jumpseed, oxeye, ironweed, wingstem. Goldenrod flushed but not open. One cottonwood seen blanching for autumn.

2003: Two dead cicadas found this morning, one on the sidewalk, one on the grass.

2004: Coming back to the porch from walking around the yard, I found a cicada, almost ready to emerge, crawling on the toe of my boot. I picked him off and set him on the apple tree. Obviously they are continuing to come out even this late in the summer.

2007: Yesterday, I noticed a mother sparrow still feeding her begging fledgling. This morning, after a night of hard rain, the zinnias have collapsed, and the purple coneflowers are bent and tattered, their color drained, their season close to over. Goldenrod gains more brightness in the alley; tall and thin-leafed coneflowers still bright full bloom; some ragweed plants have lost their pollen. More webworms seen. Japanese knotweed full. Mateo's black walnut trees continue to turn and shed.

2008: Driving from Beavercreek this morning, I noticed a number of cottonwood trees yellowing. And even though the high is supposed to reach 91 this afternoon, the air feels and smells a little like autumn. In the alley, the large, blue bindweed flowers are open along the fences. Tall coneflowers blooming but becoming tattered. Weeds are overrunning our gardens, which were well weeded before we left for Portland at the end of July. Two fireflies in the back yard as I carried the garbage cans around to the street.

2010: Overcast all day, light intermittent rain, no butterflies. Along the roads south, streaks of pale gold in the deep-green fields of soybeans, cottonwoods all turning a little, false boneset in full bloom. Picking raspberries, I looked up to see the hops in full bloom. The first flock of starlings so far in the season seen crossing the road.

2012: Faint cardinals at 5:25, Crows at 5:57, and a large, loud flock of geese flew right over the house at about 6:10. No robins heard, although the static-like sound from trigs or tree crickets makes it hard to distinguish birdcalls. Tiger swallowtail, spicebush swallowtail, giant swallowtail and a monarch noticed today at the zinnias and butterfly bushes. Several Judas maples turning. No robin or cardinal vespers, and crickets even seem a little subdued. Faint katydid calls well after dark, much less prominent than a week or so ago. A change occurring now in volume of both birds and insects.

2013: Yellow tiger swallowtails continue at the butterfly bushes. Near the covered bridge, wingstem and ironweed are full gold and purple – this would be the time to walk the South Glen for wingstem. Dozens of Italian honeybees at the hummingbird feeder are keeping the hummingbirds away. A few more peaches fell to the ground today, but the branches are still heavy with unripe fruit. On the road to Cedarville, I saw one tall maple turning red right at the top, and a flock of starlings flew in front of me north down the road past the Millers' place toward Clifton. One maple along Dayton Street is blanching. Near Lawson Place, winterberry flowers are dropping all at once. At Peggy's garden, all the gray-headed coneflowers are done blooming. Casey reports numerous tiger and zebra swallowtails and a steady passage of monarchs in his fields.

2014: A cardinal sang at 5:20 this morning, but after a few minutes, the morning turned quiet. I listened for crows and doves, but they didn't call until much later – out of sync with their summer schedule. Over night, a small variable orb-weaver, a *Neoscona crucifera*, relative of the arabesque orb-weaver (*Neoscona arabesca*), made its web between the back porch and the banana plant. This is most likely the variety I have been seeing over the years, not the arabesque. No orb-weavers yet across the shed door. And, finally, with the help of a new guidebook, I identified the long-bodied spider that weaves its horizontal web above the pond: the Long-Jawed Orb-weaver, *Tetragnatha elongata*. Four lily plants in bloom this morning, a total of four blossoms.

2015: Three lily blossoms: two rebloomers and the white Oriental. Great spangled fritillary, a monarch, golden fold-wing skippers, cabbage whites and silver spotted skippers seen in a few hours in the yard. No swallowtails noticed today or yesterday.

2016: Serviceberry leaves along Dayton Street are turning, and the first six flowers of Peggy's virgin's bower have opened. Seen in the garden: a monarch, a male swallowtail, a black swallowtail (*Papilio polyxenes*), a small checkerspot, numerous cabbage whites and silver-spotted skippers.

2017: Solar eclipse day. Faint cardinal singing at 5:25. As Jill walked down the front walk to go to work, she became tangled in a huge web of a very large orb-weaver. A monarch came to the circle garden zinnias about 7:00, the morning sun golden on the back trees and broad foliage of the castor beans.
    Two monarchs and a red admiral in the zinnias a little after noon, just before the eclipse – when the sparrows were chirping and cicadas chanting, cardinals active and vocal.
    During the eclipse, I felt the cicadas and birds become quieter, the yard became darker and burnished, as though the sun had been covered with a thin amber cloud. (My homemade eclipse

box didn't work very well, and I found it was more interesting to watch what was happening in the yard than to try to see what was happening to the sun.)

At the end of it all, I was watching three monarchs explore the zinnias. Suddenly I saw one of the monarchs swoop down toward another, and that butterfly rose to meet it and it seemed they did aerial combat for a second, soaring up and across the circle garden in tight randori, and then they returned to visiting the flowers.

Near the old peach tree (almost overshadowed by the giant pokeweed plant), the Japanese knotweed is blooming (full flower throughout the village) and the spiderwort, cut over, seems to be about to blossom once again.

Weeds glitter with dew and the long grass looks ragged, so wet and shiny. Across from the shop downtown, pink stonecrop is in early bloom, and a prairie dock plant has stalks eight-feet high, with a handful of new flowers and many buds. Along Dayton Street, the serviceberry trees are at least half bare, rust-spotted leaves on the sidewalks. In the yard, so many fragments of autumn arriving: yellow leaves of the hackberry and peach, cherry and white mulberry.

2018: Cardinal this morning at 5:15 sharp. Sun and rain, cabbage whites and a monarch and a zebra swallowtail. This evening on our walk, Jill and I heard lots of field crickets all along High Street, sometimes a space without their chirps, then spaces full of chirps.

To be alive, to move from day to day, to do the chores and greet the smiles of others is a gift and a precious blessing.

Paul Quenon

August 22nd
The 234th Day of the Year

Below Böotes thou seest the Virgin
An ear of corn held sparkling in her hand....
Her lovely tresses glow with starry light,
Stars ornament the bracelet on her hand.

Aratos

Sunrise/set: 5:53/7:22
Day's Length: 13 hours 29 minutes
Average High/Low: 83/62
Average Temperature: 72
Record High: 101 – 1936
Record Low: 47 – 1909

Weather

Today is typically drier than any day of August's final third, and it often begins a five-day period in which rain is 20 percent less likely to fall than during the rest of the month. This is also the first day of a mid-August cool spell, when afternoons in the 90s occur just ten percent of the time. However, temperatures rise to the muggy 80s sixty-five percent of the afternoons, and are in the 70s twenty-five percent of the time. Lows in the 50s cool almost half the nights on this date.

The Weather in the Week Ahead

This is the week that frost becomes possible in the northern states; snow even occurs at the upper elevations in the Rocky Mountains and in Canada. Here in the Midwest, the third major high pressure system of the month brings chances of highs in the 70s a full 40 percent of the time on August 24, the first time since July 6 that odds have been so good for milder weather.

As that cool front moves east, the period between August 25 and August 27 usually brings a return of warmer temperatures in the 80s or 90s. The 26th, 27th, 28th, and 29th each carry a 30 percent chance of highs in the 90s, and the 25th and 26th are the last days of the year on which there is only a ten to 15 percent chance of mild weather in the 70s.

On the 28th, however, the final cool wave of August approaches, and even though chances of 90s remain strong, the likelihood for chilly highs only the 60s or 70s jumps to 30 percent. August 30 is typically the coldest day of the month, and it brings a 50 percent chance of a high just in the 70s, the first time chances of that have been so good since the last day of June.

Nights in the 40s or 50s continue to occur an average of 40 percent of the time, and the morning of the 29th brings the slight possibility (a five percent chance) of light frost, for first time since the beginning of June. Chances of rain are typically 35 percent per day now, with the exception of August 28, on which date thunderstorms cross the region 65 percent of the years in my record. The 25th and 26th are usually the sunniest days this week.

Natural Calendar

August 22nd is Late Summer's Cross Quarter Day, the day on which the sun reaches halfway to autumn equinox. Almost an hour has been lost from the day's length just since the end of July, almost two hours since the year's longest days in late June.

Having dropped below the celestial equator in the first week of Late Summer, the sun now leaves the stability of Leo and enters the more volatile sign of Virgo, the first of the most violent periods of change in the second half of the year.

Throughout the remainder of the month, high Late Summer still holds sway. Cicadas and katydids and crickets are still boisterous in the night. Fold-wing skippers still chase each other in the morning sun. Great colonies of ants migrate. Beds of false boneset and trellises of virgin's bower bloom. Tall blue bellflower and burdock and euonymus keep their blossoms, and fields glow with seven-foot wingstem, tall coneflowers, early purple ironweed, late bouncing bets and black-eyed Susans.

The latest wildflowers of the year, however, the heralds of Early Fall, are set to open. Bur marigolds, zigzag goldenrod, tall goldenrod, Jerusalem artichokes, broad-leafed swamp goldenrod, New England asters and small-flowered asters are budding.

The weakening sun accelerates its message to the monarchs and swallowtails and the fall webworms. Sparrows form larger flocks. Robins emerge from their Middle Summer retreats. Great murmurations of starlings become more common. Peaches, plums, grapes, blackberries, second-crop raspberries and elderberries sweeten, then close their seasons. Yellow jackets come to feed in the fallen fruit

At the transition between Leo's vast plateau of heat and color and Libra's sudden collapse of the forest canopy, Virgo brings the first turning of the leaves and the first chance of frost to Yellow Springs. Hickory nuts, buckeyes and pecans fall to earth. The first black walnut leafturn and leafdrop began in the center of July's Leo, and now the walnut trees are shedding, yards and paths filling with their leaves. The horse chestnuts follow, and then the cottonwoods and then box elders.

Daybook

1985: Autumn starlings call in the back locust trees.

1986: Curved pods of the locusts are dry and brittle on the South Glen paths. Some maples are turning early, some buckeyes browning. Touch-me-nots keep popping. At the Covered Bridge a little blue heron seen, the size of a large crow. No cardinals heard this morning, but one sang in the middle of the afternoon. Many honeysuckle berries full red.

1987: Thoreau's note about how the blue vervain's flower stalk measures the last days of summer is still valid after a century and a half – and in Yellow Springs, Ohio, seven hundred miles southeast of Concord.

1988: Cardinal up at 5:15 a.m., then quiet

1989: Japanese knotweed bloomed today near the Covered Bridge.

1990: Pussy willow foliage falling heavily this year, beggarticks heading up, cardinals quiet. Hops deteriorating.

1991: Grackles cackle all afternoon in the back trees.

1992: A strong cold wave moved into the Northwest today. Montana had snow and temperatures in the 30s. Two hurricanes are circling in the Caribbean.

1993: Katydids were silent when I woke up this morning at 2:30. Mother cardinal feeding her baby in the cherry tree about 9:00. Still no yellow jackets here to eat the fallen apples. Goldenrod still not open.

1997: Horseweed is just opening. White snakeroot is coming in, but behind its usual timetable. Yellow wingstem and primrose are still fresh. Goldenrod looks to be a week or ten days from flowering. Pokeberries are late turning purple. The violet resurrection lilies and phlox that announced the start of August have held a bit longer than they sometimes do.

1998: Cardinal sings at 5:27, then jays and crows by 5:30, wren at 6:00. First brown Asian ladybug seen at the pond. As showy coneflowers die back along the south wall, goldenrod is opening. Trees deteriorate, paling and dropping leaves rapidly as the late-summer drought intensifies.

1999: A few fireflies still, the intensity of their season stretched by the drought. Starlings clucking in the trees all day.

2000: Both crows and cardinals this morning at 5:30. Have the crows moved in now for the next six or seven months, their calls the earliest, or synchronous with the cardinals' until middle spring? Bodies of cicadas here and there around the yard. They still chant through the afternoons, but their autumn dying is underway. Black walnuts on the street yesterday morning.

2001: Several full blooming patches of resurrection lilies near Wilmington. But north in Yellow Springs, all the lilies are gone.

2002: One red admiral butterfly seen today, one monarch, one Eastern black swallowtail.

2003: Several monarchs seen on Kelleys Island today.

2004: A monarch and a great spangled fritillary in the north garden today. The yearling redbud along the west border has lost maybe a fifth of its leaves to a fungus or attack, probably verticillium wilt, a fatal disease. There are also sticky white mealy-bug-type scales on the trunk. The resurrection lilies are gone at Mrs. Lawson's place and along the south garden border.

2007: I heard a screech owl this morning in the back trees at 5:15. Robins chirped a little at 5:22 until a cardinal called at 5:33, then silence. Rain continues heavy throughout the Midwest, the drought clearly over for the time being. No birds at the feeder at all this morning.

2008: The stonecrop started to open yesterday, small pink flowers, and the first of Peggy's virgin's bower unfolded. Resurrection lilies are still in full bloom at Don's and other properties. Local corn shows stress from this month's lack of rain. Blue jays active near the alley this morning and yesterday morning.

2010: The sun is back, the barometer up past 30.00, and the butterflies have returned: tiger swallowtails, spicebush swallowtails, Eastern black swallowtails, fritillaries, monarchs, skippers.

2011: First morning below 60 degrees in what seems like two months! Cardinal at 5:30 to about 5:45, crows late at about 5:55. High trilling crickets from the time I got up until they were lost in the calls of the cicadas. In the alley, tall coneflowers gone, blue bindweed full, pokeweed purple, resurrection lilies going very fast. Saw two tiger swallowtails, two monarchs (and Jeanie saw several more on her drive), one spicebush or black swallowtail, one polygonia, many cabbage whites and silver-spotted skippers, one common buckeye in maybe an hour total outside. Hummingbird moths continue to visit the butterfly bush, as well. Four buds remain on our last orange day lily.

2012: Another chilly morning in the 50s. Faint cardinals heard at 5:20 a.m. Many Judas maples seen on the way in to Kettering and especially in the city itself, a pronounced coloration.

2013: Doves heard before 5:30 this morning. The serviceberry trees along Dayton Street are losing brown leaves like the black walnut trees. Don's sidewalk is lined with the fallen foliage. One very late Star Gazer lily opened over night in the north garden near the peach tree.

2014: Three yellow reblooming lilies in the yard today, resurrection lilies finally gone here, but a few still open around town. The beggarticks on the northwest side of the porch are budding now, and the arrowhead in the pond has finished blooming. Outside today for a short time, just saw one sulphur and many cabbage whites. In John Bryan Park, a brief walk at the Gorge trailhead, a subdued habitat of old mint and scraggly daisy fleabane, a few touch-me-nots, and an undergrowth of budded white snakeroot, only a few plants blooming. The Indian tobacco, *lobelia inflate*, which I thought was a rare Ohio orchid at the end of July, had just completed its flower cycle, small seedpods round and fat. One firefly seen near the front porch tonight.

2015: Prairie dock still in full bloom at the south end of High Street. A fat orb-weaver has set up in a corner of the front porch. Three lilies today: a couple of rebloomers and the last petals of the white stargazer. Marcie came by the store while I was working, said she had heard a bobwhite outside her home on Omar Circle about a week ago. Fits with what Barbara and Michele reported.

2016: One monarch and many skippers and cabbage whites today. Some white snakeroot in bloom at Bryan Park, most just budded.

2017: A monarch came to the circle garden zinnias about 7:00, the morning sun golden on the back trees and broad foliage of the castor beans. Jill saw another monarch this afternoon near her house. Near the old peach tree (almost overshadowed by the giant pokeweed plant), the Japanese knotweed is blooming (full flower throughout the village) and the spiderwort, cut over, seems to be about to blossom once again. Weeds glitter with dew and the long grass looks ragged, so wet and shiny. Across from the shop downtown, pink stonecrop is in early bloom, and a prairie dock plant has stalks eight-feet high, with a handful of new flowers and many buds. Along Dayton Street, the serviceberry trees are at least half bare, rust-spotted leaves on the sidewalks. In the yard, so many fragments of autumn arriving: yellow leaves of the hackberry and peach, cherry and white mulberry.

2018: Cool and bright, light breeze, cabbage whites swarming around the jumpseed flowers, four monarchs, a spicebush swallowtail and an Eastern black and a hummingbird in the zinnias, braving the wind, swooping around me, indulging in the colors and blooms. This evening, gibbous moon almost full, a brief cardinal vespers, the temperature at 61 degrees, and the katydids began calling about a half hour later than they did a couple of days ago. One firefly seen.

Every day is a journey, and the journey itself is home.

Basho

August 23rd
The 235th Day of the Year

For you the light dispels the darkness; for you the sun, moon, and stars shed their light; for you the earth bears flowers and trees and fruits; for you the air and earth and waters are all filled with marvelous life – all so that earthly life may not be sad and make you blind to the joy of eternity.

Peter Chrysologus

Sunrise/set: 5:54/7:21
Day's Length: 13 hours 33 minutes
Average High/Low: 83/62
Average Temperature: 72
Record High: 99 – 1898
Record Low: 44 – 1888

Weather

There is a 15 percent chance of highs in the 90s today, a 50 percent chance of a high in the 80s and a 35 percent chance of a high in the 70s. Rain comes three years in a decade. Five nights in ten go below 60 degrees, a percentage that signals a definitive break with Dog Day weather, and another step towards winter.

Natural Calendar

Natural history easily becomes a litany of turning points in the progress of the year. Each day brings out more corners in the apparently straight, uniform road of the seasons. With an inventory of leaves and flowers and sounds, the elusive present emerges briefly in the spaces between the past and future.

In cooler afternoons, the wind becomes more pungent, sweeter, sharper, maybe from apples down or peach drop, maybe from the woods and undergrowth aging, mellowing as Cross-Quarter Day approaches. When the air is wet and thick, fogs form in the hollows before dawn.

Buckeyes and black walnuts and Osage fruits are heavy on their branches. Green acorns are browning, brittle in their clusters. In the woods, lopseed and panicled tick trefoil are fading, white snakeroot blooming, jumpseeds jumping, touch-me-nots popping, Virginia creeper and sumac reddening sometimes this early.

Skunk cabbage has decayed, and the swamps are littered with its stalks near the purple loosestrife and the great pink water mallow and the American lotus. Most of the sycamore bark has fallen, shedding near completion for the year. Japanese knotweed is budding. Crab apples have all ripened in city parks. Yellow sow thistles line the roads, blue chicory, deep violet ironweed, golden wingstem, silver Queen Anne's lace beside them.

The bird and insect clocks strike Late Summer through the week. When the days are sunny and mild, all the butterflies visit the gardens: monarchs, brown, buckeyes, swallowtails, skippers, cabbage whites, sulphurs, red admirals, painted ladies, polygonias.

Now it is too late for pre-dawn robinsong, and cardinals wait to sing until a quarter past six in the morning (more than an hour past their summer solstice time). Doves join briefly a few minutes later, blue jays and red-bellied woodpeckers maybe ten minutes after doves. Then come the crows, and then cicadas take the place of almost all the birds throughout the day.

Katydids and crickets begin their chants when cicadas rest at dusk. The katydids often stop their rasping calls hours before sunup; crickets sing until morning twilight. Through the night, only an occasional firefly tells of Middle Summer.

Daybook

1982: Tonight, only scattered fireflies. Grackles are becoming more noticeable in the afternoons.

1983: Madison, Wisconsin: Many of the wildflowers are at the same stage as in Ohio: burdock, motherwort, goosefoot, white snakeroot, wild lettuce, ragweed, bull thistles. Some remnants from June and July: a little white sweet clover, and some daisy fleabane.

1985: Jimson weed seen full bloom in Mad River.

1986: One cardinal sings at 7:30 a.m. In the swamp, a few large-flowered bidens are opening. Some new foliage of sweet rocket has started.

1987: After two weeks in Indiana, I returned home to clearweed in full bloom, some purple pokeweed berries, Japanese knotweed budding, boneset full bloom. Yellow jackets, absent most of the summer, were all over the fallen apples. No cardinals heard today.

1988: Geese flew over at 7:30 p.m.

1991: Grackles in the back trees this afternoon. Cardinal sings sporadically, blue jay seen but not heard.

1993: Definite decline in the yellow coneflowers today, about half a dozen wilting. resurrection lilies also wilting quickly.

1998: Pussy willow leaves maybe a third fallen to the yard. Black walnut leaves half gone in some places.

1999: The frog in the pond has been quiet for several days now.

2000: Snakes in the north yard, but none seen near the pond since June. In the east garden, the stonecrop has started to open. Along the freeway east and on some back roads, the tall goldenrod has turned. The first small white asters are blooming against the south wall.

2001: Rain this morning, and I listened in the dark from 5:00 to 6:15 : not a single birdcall.

2002: Tiger swallowtail at 7:05 a.m. Doves, cardinals, jays off and on throughout the day.

2003: Kelleys Island in Lake Erie: Robins begin to chirping 5:10 a.m., are actively moving around the campground by 5:20. A large flock of blackbirds arrived, like it did yesterday morning, at 5:50. Cormorants flew over at 6:00. The gulls came in to scavenge just a few minutes later. As people woke up and started moving around, the birds disappeared. Half a dozen monarchs seen on the drive from the island to Yellow Springs.

2004: Between Yellow Springs and Wilberforce, the land is rusting, turning towards fall. The cornfields are gold and green, and so many trees are coloring early. My ash at school, always ahead of other trees, has a few yellow leaves, reflecting patches of ashes and locusts and lindens throughout the area. At the Mills Lawn Park, one black walnut is completely bare.

2006: Just a faint blush on the bittersweet at the corner of Limestone and High. At South College and High, the prairie dock is still in full bloom. A tree cricket seen in the bathroom tonight, a pale, thin katydid-like creature.

2008: No cardinal song this morning or yesterday morning. A slight darkening to Don's burning bush along the alley. Webworms cut from the west redbud this afternoon; the worms had begun to emerge from some of their webs. Golden fold-wing skippers play in the sun through the day.

2010: In the alley at 6:15 this morning, the breeze was chilly for the first time in at least a month. The air was rich with the smell of windfall apples. In the countryside, many cornfields have become golden, their leaves drying out. Butterflies still visit the zinnias and butterfly bushes, but they seem to be thinning out. The first jumpseeds from Moya's yard are brittle, jumping.

2011: Two browns seen, but no swallowtails at the butterfly bushes today. Jeanie did see two monarchs when she was driving to Beavercreek.

2012: Silver olive shrubs along the freeway have patches of gold.

2013: Japanese knotweed full bloom in the Phillips Street alley, virgin's bower and white autumn allium full throughout the village. Male tiger swallowtail butterflies still common in the butterfly bushes and the zinnias, and I saw a monarch when I crossed Dayton Street in the afternoon.

2014: Outside for just a short time today: one monarch, one yellow tiger, many cabbage whites playing, mating. The knotweed, virgin's bower, white autumn allium are full, just like last year at this time. Joe Pye is more than half to seed, some of the false boneset is finally open, and the phlox are almost all gone, the violets and the whites.

2015: At sunrise, to the buzz of tree crickets: intermittent crows, a peeping robin, steady mourning dove, one cardinal. The morning chorus over for sure. In the yard, all the heliopsis is gone now, the phlox weakening, Joe Pye mostly gray, the false boneset absent – did not make my transplanting this past spring – a few evening primrose blossoms, a reblooming lily and the white star gazer. And I thought the giant hibiscus had ended its season, but I had forgotten to look closely, and this morning, it had two new deep red flowers seven inches in diameter. Two New England asters noticed open downtown – where I saw Rick and Mary; they had heard a bobwhite last week, supporting other reports I've had. In the yard, I keep running into orb-weavers and micrathenas. Jonatha sent a photo she took yesterday of a tiger moth caterpillar.

2016: Two hackberry butterflies in the north garden this morning, perhaps a late-summer hatch. One azure, many skippers and cabbage whites. At Mills Lawn, the black walnut trees have kept their leaves so far, only one bright yellow patch of gold in one of them. This afternoon: a yellow swallowtail, an Eastern black, a monarch, a polygonia.

2017: A major cool wave, the offspring of the new moon, perigee and the August 24 front, has settled across the Valley now after yesterday's storm, the cool expected to stay for days. One monarch in the north zinnias at 9:25 this morning, and then it seemed (that is, if it really was the same monarch) to stay all day, was still circling around the yard visiting zinnias and then flying to the redbud tree, then floating down and back and around. I saw two silver-spotted skippers as I watched the show. Along Dayton Street now, some Japanese knotweed in full bloom. At the women's park, all the coneflowers have faded, but rudbeckia, cup plant and several other varieties keep color amid the tattered coneflowers. At John Bryan Park, Jill and I saw a fawn with its mother walking together in the river shallows. The fawn had lost almost all its spots.

2018: First morning in the 50s, sun and dew, moon at apogee but two days from full. Daisies down to one blossom, heliopsis to a handful, jumpseeds thinning quickly. Monarchs continue in the garden, one male tiger swallowtail, many cabbage whites, one skipper, many smaller bumblebees. Katydids began at 7:49, in spite of the cool evening temperatures. Geese flew over honking at 8:00.

Why do we love them, these last days of something
Like summer, of freedom to move in few clothes,
Though frost has flattened the morning grass?
They tell us we shall live forever. Stretched
Like a rainbow across day's end, my shadow
Makes a path from my feet; I am my path.

John Updike

August 24th
The 236th Day of the Year

The base of the leaf was yellowish green, but along the sides and tip it was tinted with peach and rose - and this was only the end of August.. I tucked the lone leaf carefully into my wallet. It would remind me to be aware while summer was slipping away.

Sigurd Olson

Sunrise/set: 5:55/7:19
Day's Length: 13 hours 24 minutes
Average High/Low: 82/62
Average Temperature: 72
Record High: 99 – 1903
Record Low: 44 – 1902

Weather

Under the influence of the third major high-pressure system of the month, today brings chances of highs in the cool 70s forty percent of the time, the first time since July 6th that odds have been so good for milder weather. Temperatures warm to the 80s forty-five percent of the time, however, with 90s occurring 15 percent of the afternoons. Rain comes one year in three. Clouds cover the sky four years in ten. Nighttime lows fall below 60 forty percent of the time.

Natural Calendar

The lowering sun accelerates its message to the monarchs and swallowtails, to the fall webworms and to the Hickory Horned Devils (the caterpillars of the *Citheronia regalis* moth). It is high Late Summer: Beds of false boneset and trellises of virgin's bower break into bloom. Tall blue bellflower and burdock and euonymus keep their blossoms, and fields glow with seven-foot wingstem, tall coneflowers, early purple ironweed, late bouncing bets and black-eyed Susans. The autumn crop of raspberries darkens.

The latest flowers of the season are getting set to open. Bur marigolds, zigzag goldenrod, tall goldenrod, Jerusalem artichokes, broad-leafed swamp goldenrod and small-flowered asters are budding. Plums and grapes and elderberries sweeten. Insects still are everywhere. Cicadas and katydids and crickets are still loud. Fold-wing skippers still chase each other in the morning sun.

The very first of the black walnut leaf turn and leafdrop began in the middle of Leo, and now the walnut trees are quickly yellowing. Yards and paths fill with their leaves. Sometimes the black walnut trees are completely bare by the first days of September. The horse chestnuts follow, then the cottonwoods, then box elders. Judas maples, betraying the messiah of June with red and orange, foretell October.

Yellow jackets come to feed in the fallen fruit, and great colonies of ants often begin migration. Murmurations of starlings sweep over the fields, and long flocks of grackles and blackbirds follow the harvest. Robins congregate in the woodlots, gathering for migration. Peaches, blackberries, second-crop raspberries, plums and elderberries sweeten, then close their seasons. Hickory nuts, buckeyes and pecans fall to earth.

Daybook

1982: Some leaves are turning on our northeast maple. Throughout town, a few sumac, box elder, elms and sycamores have shades of yellow and brown. Field thistles are blooming along King Street.

1990: Giant hyssop in late full bloom along Grinnell Road. I noticed it starting maybe two weeks ago.

1992: Sunday morning, barometer steady at 30.34, temperature 66 degrees, humidity 55 percent, sky mostly overcast, scattered fog: I ride down the new bike path toward Goes Station. On both sides of the right-of-way, protected from cutting by steep banks and ditches: intermittent pasture habitats, roadside habitats, wetland habitats, woodland habitats. The corridor opens a cross-section of the county flora, reveals the pace and the character of the season.

Some things are late this cool year. July's horseweed is just opening. White snakeroot is way behind its usual timetable. Yellow wingstem and primrose, which provide most of the gold to my ride, are still fresh and strong. Purple ironweed, with the brightest corymbs of the trip, is at its peak. Tall bellflowers, a consistent violet blue from Yellow Springs south to the Little Miami bridge, are holding as though it still were Middle Summer. Goldenrod, often blooming by the 13th, looks to be a week or ten days from flowering.

Some pasture plants stay on from June: red clovers, white sweet clover, scattered yellow sweet clover, daisy fleabane, sweet rockets out of time, wood sorrel, white campion. But most of the way, it's still July and early August: Queen Anne's lace, Japanese knotweed, thin-leafed coneflowers, cattails, floppy soapwort, boneset, false boneset, yellow moth mullein, soft pale and spotted touch-me-nots, a little wood mint, a few bergamot, great yellow hyssop, one rare cardinal flower, rough Jerusalem artichoke, white bindweed, climbing wild cucumber, shy downy skullcap, goosefoot, the tallest field thistles – some ten feet high with racemes two to three feet across, behemoth, shrub-like burdocks – some still blossoming.

1993: No birds singing before dawn. Katydids quiet in the very early morning, and then one heard at 4:45 for a few minutes, then only crickets. Monarchs have been common for the past week, and two even flew in front of the car yesterday when I was driving home from school. Swallowtails have been increasing in numbers throughout August.

1998: Baby wrens in the front yard still huddle in their nest. No morning bird chorus these days. A cardinal called a few times at 5:33 a.m., a crow at 5:40.

1999: Hurricane season is in full swing now, the last week creating three. One went across Texas south into Mexico. The others are moving towards the East Coast.

2001: Skunk odor under the house this morning, following a week of sightings and smells. Katydids still heard at 3:00 a.m., silence soon afterwards. Whistling crickets, making a sound like a dull, long police whistle, were the most prominent singers. Chirping field crickets were calling off and on at 5:00 a.m. First cardinal at 5:55.

2003: Cardinal at 5:15 a.m., continuing on and off until close to 6:00. Doves still calling. Resurrection lilies are still in bloom in Yellow Springs. One last daylily flowering. The first New England aster seen. Purple coneflowers are tattered and well past their prime. The golden rudbeckia are in full bloom but the first of their blossoms have started to shrivel. One firefly seen tonight.

2004: One monarch came to the zinnias this afternoon.

2005: Henry reported clusters of frog eggs in his small pond today.

2006: Skunks continue to spray in the neighborhood close to our house almost every night. Cardinal at 5:29 a.m. and again about ten minutes later. Then silence. One wren chattered at daybreak. False boneset opened in the yard on the 23rd. Peaches are sweet but still a little hard.

2007: Chickadees, nuthatches, titmice and cardinals dominate the bird feeder this morning, sparrows taking a back row to the songbirds. Mateo's black walnut tree is now down to about half of its leaves. Euonymus berries are full size, big as honeysuckle berries. The tall, white flowers of late August hostas dominate Moya's yard. Monarchs and swallowtails are common in the garden. Showy coneflowers are starting to die back in Don's front yard. Our black-eyed Susans are still in full bloom. Cicadas are still strong, start early (about 7:00 a.m.) in this long, humid hot spell.

2008: Late August heat and drought continue as I make late inventory: two orange day lilies have opened since we got back from visiting Jeni in Portland; mallow is down to just a few flowers; one red rose on the new bush, full pink roses on the old; Queen Anne's lace has contracted; oakleaf hydrangea flowers have become a dark brown-pink; false boneset is well budded; the September "Hillbilly" hostas have come in; still no buds on the Jerusalem artichokes or the New England asters; rose of Sharon still in bloom; showy coneflowers and black-eyed Susans hold, and some faded purple coneflowers; some of the short bellflowers Jeanie planted in July continue to flower; the Heliopsis patch fills almost the whole northwest garden.

2009: Chicory thinning along Limestone Street. Webworms in one of the crab apple trees at the park. Giant hibiscus still full bloom around the back porch. At the Cincinnati Zoo, crepe myrtles in full bloom.

2010: Screech owl at 5:09, robins at 5:19, cardinals at 5:27, crows at 5:33 this morning. Monarchs, tiger swallowtails, Eastern blacks, skippers at the butterfly bush today, but not in the numbers of a week or so ago. A full bowl of raspberries picked this morning, the fruit of three days. Crickets loud when I walked Bella tonight.

2011: The very first flower on Peggy's virgin's bower opened last night. At night, neighborhood swept with sound: katydids, chirping field crickets, high steady trills, intermittent trills and steady, grinding calls of the tree crickets.

2012: Screech owl, ghostly call at 4:00 this morning. Only faint cardinals around 5:30, then crows. Trigs still calling at 7:00. On the way to Dayton, a marked increase in coloration from cottonwoods, maples, silver olives, locusts, ashes, a rapid change since last week.

2013: Four tiger swallowtails and a great spangled fritillary at one time in the back butterfly bushes this morning. The first ripe peach fell to the ground. I ate it on the spot; the windfalls have begun now. This afternoon an Eastern black swallowtail in the zinnias. Prairie dock still at the peak of its bloom at the corner of West South College and High Street.

2014: A dove was the first bird to call this morning, 5:30; a cardinal just a couple of minutes later, then crows, then a robin singong – but isolated, not in chorus; then several blue jays, and then the sharp cries of a red-tailed hawk.

2015: Early morning after a night rain, calm and cool 50s, pure clear blue gray sky: static from the tree crickets, intermittent calls of the whistling crickets; the first cardinals right at 5:30, continuing for several minutes. Crows at exactly 5:35, a dove heard through the noise of cars from the street at 5:45. Finches chirring near dawn, some sparrow chatter a little later.

No robins. In the garden, one lone reblooming lily and the white stargazer. One monarch at about 8:00, then two more and a yellow tiger seen through the morning. Above the zinnias and tithonias, a cascade, a wall of Japanese knotweed, their best year ever, and above them, the hops vines that have taken over the honeysuckles are heavy with blossoms. A soft blush has appeared on the bittersweet above the gate to High Street. At the covered bridge, wingstem and touch-me-nots and ironweed tall and full field thistles as lush as I've ever seen them. Along the river path, wood nettle is getting ragged, but it is still troublesome. As I drove home from downtown: a gust full of black walnut leaves.

2016: Fewer butterflies, it seems, but one new very black swallowtail, no blue on its tail.

2017: Jill saw three monarchs on her trip to Delaware, Ohio. I only noticed a couple of silver-spotted skippers in the garden, in spite of the perfect weather: sun and mild. I almost stepped on two toads in the grass this afternoon: migration time?

2018: One cardinal call at 5:15 a.m., then quiet. Crows calling when I went out at 6:30. Doves still sing through the morning. Jeanie's white Stargazer lily continues in bloom. A blush on the goldenrod along King Street, the panicled dogwood berries creamy white. I noticed in the daybook from August's past that the screech owl has not called in the yard since Jeanie died. This evening, the katydids came in early at 8:35, in the middle of a full range of cricket songs. Then I woke up at 2:00 the next morning, they had stopped calling.

What is easier to discuss mutually with You, O God, the three crows that flew by in the sun with the light flashing on their rubber wings. Or the sunlight coming quietly through the cracks in the boards. Or the crickets in the grass?

Thomas Merton

August 25th
The 237th Day of the Year

The Earth's changing relationship to the Sun quietly turns the color of the landscape, creating intervals of time out of matter, sequence from leaves and flowers.

bf

Sunrise/set: 5:56/7:18
Day's Length: 13 hours 22 minutes
Average High/Low: 82/61
Average Temperature: 72
Record High: 99 – 1903
Record Low: 48 – 1891

Weather

As the third major cool front of the month moves east, the period between August 25th and August 27th often brings a return of warmer temperatures. Chances of highs in the 90s double over yesterday's chances, rise from 15 percent to 30 percent. Warm 80s come 60 percent of the afternoons, with cooler 70s only occurring ten percent of the time. Showers pass through Yellow Springs around three years in ten, but the sun shines most of the day. (This is historically one of the clearest days in August.) Half the nights provide pleasant sleeping in the 50s.

Natural Calendar

Judas trees betray the Christ of summer, patches of gold showing on the Osage and cottonwoods and poplars and maples, kisses of scarlet on creeper and poison ivy. Panicled dogwood has its first white berries. Dogbane pods have grown to ten inches now and a few are turning red. Wood nettle, tall nettle and small-flowered agrimony have gone to black seeds. Buckeye leaves are browning, walnut trees weathering and shedding. Redbuds and burning bush are blushing. Mint has reached the close of its cycle, teasel is complete, and coneflowers are fading.

The Stars

The house-shaped star group, Cepheus, has moved into the middle of the sky by midnight, marking the start of Early Fall. To the east of Cepheus, find the zigzag formation of Cassiopeia, followed by Perseus (looking vaguely like a horse) rising in the northeast. The Big Dipper continues to hug the northern horizon throughout the night.

Daybook

1983: Bees everywhere through South Glen, sometimes five or six on a single golden wingstem plant. Yellow leafcup, ironweed, tall coneflower, field thistle, white snakeroot, touch-me-not, great blue lobelia full bloom still. Fog fruit discovered. Goldenrod flushed but not open yet. Brown brome grass and parsnips, hops done blooming. Jumpseed mostly gone to seed, wood nettle drooping, Joe Pye weed graying, ragweed heavy with pollen, oxeye fading. Everything I notice is a sign of September.

1984: Geese restless, flying near 6:00 this morning. First beggarticks bloomed today.

1985: Honeysuckle berries have turned dark orange in the last week or so.

1986: Grinnell swamp: Blue lobelias still full. Goldenrod has just started here and out toward South Glen. Tick trefoil burs stick to my pants, one more autumn step.

1987: On a rainy afternoon, 65 degrees, the crickets were subdued, bees hiding in their hives, cardinals silent. The weathering of the leaves was accentuated by the drizzle and gray sky, Judas maples seemed brighter. A few buckeyes had split their shells over night.

1988: Maples in the yard are still completely green. The drought has not accelerated fall coloring yet.

1990: Cardinals quiet most of the day. Buckeye leaves turning very quickly now. Field thistles are in full bloom, have been for a week or so. Goldenrod is flushed but none seen completely open around

Yellow Springs. Late August fogs arriving, humidity higher, making morning temperatures seem sharper. The basil smell of Late Summer so strong this year.

1992: Across the county, cottonwoods, ash, maple are turning, patches of yellow and red, rusting, fading. Branches of honey locusts bright gold. At my office window, the small ash tree, which is always the first tree to lose its leaves, is maybe a fifth gone and deteriorating quickly. It will be bare in a couple of weeks.

1993: Showy coneflowers dying back more quickly, another dozen or so wilted over night. First yellow jacket seen today. They are probably late because the past six weeks have been so dry. Gilbert White notes the connection between hornets and rain in his 18th-century journal.

1999: The red sedum has been opening for several days now. Russian sage still strong in the yard and around town. The ironweed and the butterfly bush hold on, solid purple additions to the north garden – but we need dozens more for late August. Heliopsis is going quickly, phlox is almost gone, and flax has disappeared. In the pond, the pickerel plant has a last flower, the purple loosestrife has come to the end of its spikes. Arrowhead is still open, but most of the stalks are leaning over to seed into the water. Showy coneflowers are two-thirds wilted. On the picnic table, the winter tomato plants in their pots look strong, some of them almost a foot high. Beside them, the honeysuckle berries are turning orange. One firefly seen after dark.

2000: Rumination on my inventories: Grounding in just what lies around me, learning to accept home, the solitude of landscape, finding enough in the most simple observations, embracing the ordinary and expecting nothing more, accepting this particular passage of time, salvation in the commonplace, the measurement of the dragon fly, the measurement of the goldenrod, asking nothing more than these plain acts, allowing, opening, watching the finite visions that contain no transcendence or special compensation, considering the precision of each fragment that names the exact place of Earth's orbit and my exact place within it.

2001: Crickets strong at 5:00 this morning, then fade with dawn. Blue jay at 5:36. Cardinal and crows at 5:37. Chatter of a wren, one call only at 5:47. Doves at 5:57. After that, only sporadic singing. Fireflies are completely gone now.

2002: At 4:30 this morning, only crickets. By 5:20, the crickets fading and then cardinals beginning. Throughout the Yellow Springs gardens, rapid decline of late spring perennials: ironweed half gone, only remnants of phlox, heliopsis, butterfly bush. The dying maple in front of the house is a third turned already. Several monarchs seen today, and a pearl-crescent skipper, a European skipper, and fiery skipper. At South Glen, the first goldenrod is starting.

2003: To southeastern Ohio: Joe Pye still full, goldenrod starting, Jerusalem artichokes seen, wingstem, ironweed, jewelweed bright. Many cottonwoods beginning to yellow, many black walnuts almost bare. Probably a dozen monarchs seen on the drive. At home near suppertime, I found one more monarch in the ironweed and another in the butterfly bush. Greg came across three "hickory horned devils," caterpillars of the *Citheronia regalis* moth, when he was working in Xenia.

2005: To central Ohio, Amish country: The fields and hills were deep green throughout the drive. A number of cornfields showed stress from the scarcity of rain, but the soybeans were strong, and most corn seemed in at least fair condition. Wingstem was the dominant flowering plant throughout, with sundrops, ironweed, Joe Pye weed common. Some goldenrod was blooming, but most was only flushed. No monarchs seen. At home, virgin's bower is fully budded, Japanese knotweed in bloom, stonecrop just starting to show pink.

2006: Stonecrop opened on the 24th. Screech owl this morning at 4:30, called for a few minutes, then silence. Katydids stopped by 3:00 a.m.

2008: Only faint cardinal calls in the distance this morning about 5:40. But a flock of geese flew over the house around 7:00 – the first time I have heard morning geese in a while. In the alley, more apples are falling. In Beavercreek, I noticed a red maple turning and several ashes turning gold. On the way to Xenia, false boneset is in full bloom, goldenrod flushed but only a few plants opening. I weeded along the north side of the house, and I cut back hosta stalks and rusted ferns. In the south garden, I dug up the purple loosestrife and placed it near the peach trees (peaches turning now, but still very hard – although the Pennsylvania peaches we bought last week at the farmers' market were perfect. As I was walking Bella this evening, a small skunk crossed Dayton Street in front of us.

Reading over past entries, I can see that such a complete transformation has taken place in August. It is the kind of change that I sometimes tend to ignore because of the heat and the days that are still quite long. There are still enough flowers in bloom to distract from the flowers that are gone. The high canopy remains deep green, betrayed only slightly by the red maples, the cottonwoods and black walnuts.

2009: Mateo's goldenrod starting to open.

2010: Robins faintly at 5:16, cardinal at 5:21, no crows heard this morning. To the Athens, Ohio area in the afternoon: short goldenrod, Joe Pye weed, field thistles in full bloom (Joe Pye weed to seed at home for at least ten days). Many cornfields brown. Two small flocks of starlings seen.

2011: Cardinal at 5:35 a.m., then quiet. To Hocking Hills in southeastern Ohio: Lots of Joe Pye seen along the way. The crops were strong throughout the ride, the soybeans especially, fields of deep forest-green beans, the leaves turned up like whitecaps in the southwest wind. Goldenrod started coming in as we approached the foothill country past Chillicothe. At the park, bouncing bets, tansy, Queen Anne's lace, chicory, wingstem, ironweed, jewel weed, jump seed (not jumping), milkweed all to pods, purple knapweed all around the campground. At Rose Lake, many large dragonflies with powder-blue tipped wings. Occasional tiger swallowtails seen, and many dark swallowtails crossing the road, probably spicebush swallowtails. Only one monarch seen on the trip.

2012: Jeanie heard the ominous call of the screech owl this morning (her birthday morning) about 3:00. Only trigs calling when I went out at 5:20. Cardinal at 5:35 a.m., almost at the same time as the crows. Several monarchs, many hummingbird moths, a giant swallowtail, a polydamas swallowtail, a spicebush swallowtail. A red admiral, and many yellow tiger swallowtails along with cabbage whites, a brown, and a sulphur in the zinnias and butterfly bush within about two hours time this morning. Finches, still very gold, at the feeders all day. First tall goldenrod seen in bloom at DeWine's pond, no others open throughout the local countryside. Sunflower fields around town still in full bloom.

2013: Walking Bella at 5:30 this morning, clear and cool: distant cardinals and then crows. No doves calling. Strong thrips and some field crickets, no whistling crickets or katydids. A monarch and a sulphur in the zinnias when I came back from church. Now the heliopsis is all gone, the phlox with only scattered blooms.

    On the walking meditation this afternoon, low goldenrod was flowering in under the canopy, and white snakeroot was in very early bloom. Buds had formed on the zigzag goldenrod. Leaves trickled down, and the path seemed louder, with a few leaves now crisp underfoot. The upper foliage of one maple had turned. In town, Tim's black walnut tree was totally bare. Sunset at Ellis Pond: arrowhead and jewelweed in full bloom.

2014: The orb-weaver is back, its web covering the top half of the shed door. When she saw me coming, she retreated up into the shed. One male tiger and one giant swallowtail seen during brief outings in the yard. The first two gladioli I planted so late are blooming by the pond.

2015: Cool and clear: Cardinal at 5:24 a.m., crows at 5:30.

2016: One ragged black swallowtail at the zinnias, many silver-spotted skippers – up to five at a time in the tithonias, some mating, many cabbage whites fluttering in and out of randori. Boneset fading across from the Covered Bridge. Inventory in the honeysuckle and locust tangles of South Glen: late but prominent wingstem and ironweed along the river and lining the paths, drifts of tall coneflowers not far from my old fishing hole, full blooming leafcup, one Deptford pink, one field thistle, most wood nettle all gone to seed, the very first tall goldenrod coming into bloom, a blue lobelia, a few tall bell flowers, budded white snakeroot, common ragweed to seed, all the milkweed I used to see near the old barn now covered with goldenrod ready to open, the ground being taken over by smartweed. A great spangled fritillary seen and one bedraggled black swallowtail – almost gray. One side of my pants legs full of small burrs.

2017: Another bright, cool day: one monarch, one male tiger swallowtail, one small black swallowtail. Goldenrod is almost blooming at Jill's. A few more spiderworts come open; I should cut them back quite early past their best. In the woods, at the high path, some lobelias, some snakeroot, some bell flowers, a last agrimony, very still. A huge patch of great ragweed in Clifton: all of its pollen seeming to be gone. Hurricane Harvey, Category 4, strikes the Texas coast this evening, the first landfall hurricane of the season.

2018: Mild and a little muggy this morning. When Jill and I went outside at 5:35, a cardinal was singing, and he continued until the crows came in at 5:55, and then I heard a dove at 6:00, and then a chickadee. The high static of tree crickets remained constant through the night into the day, and I heard field crickets throughout our walk at sunrise. Katydids started at 8:45 this evening, the streets shining after the storm at 6:00.

You will find much more laboring amongst the woods than you ever will amongst books. Woods and stones will teach you what you can never hear from any master.

Bernard of Clairvaux

August 26th
The 238th Day of the Year

Already swallows are moving down from the north. I saw them ranged side by side on telephone wires this morning. In the circle of the seasons, there is no pause. Already summer slides toward autumn. On this hot afternoon, at the very summit of the season, signs of change are in the air.

Edwin Way Teale

Sunrise/set: 5:57/7:16
Day's Length: 13 hours 19 minutes
Average High/Low: 82/61
Average Temperature: 72
Record High: 96 – 1948
Record Low: 47 – 1945

Weather

There is only a 15 percent chance of highs to remain in the mild 70s today. Eighties are most common, occurring 55 percent of the afternoon. Nineties come frequently too — 30 percent of the time. Chances of precipitation continue at late August's typical 25 to 30 percent, and sun almost always dominates the clouds. Evenings are cool, below 60 half the time.

Natural Calendar

The last week of August brings the peak of Purple Pokeweed Berry Season in the alleyways, Beggartick Flowering Season in the garden, Bur Marigold Season in the wetlands. Burrs of the tick trefoil stick to hikers' stockings and pants legs as Tick Trefoil Burr Season begins. Hickory Nutting Season spreads across the forest floor.

Daybook

1982: Tips of the maple in the yard are starting to turn. Almost all the fireflies have disappeared.

1983: Most fireflies gone.

1984: South Glen: Jumpseeds and touch-me-nots full bloom in the woods. Ragweed, oxeye, heal-all, showy coneflowers, wingstem, and ironweed full in the fields. Some white snakeroot fading. Many milkweed pods fully developed, and some wood nettle flowers have turned to green seed clusters. All the white vervain is gone. Hickory nuts common on the path now. Pokeweed berries are dark and soft. Golden patches of linden along the roadsides. Sedge has withered. Some brown acorns seen. At the covered bridge, red smartweed, burdock, a few tall bellflowers, agrimony, hog peanuts, wild lettuce flowering. Asters budding.

1987: Bittersweet scent of old apples in the damp, heavy night. Cygnus, the Northern Cross, overhead in the clear night sky.

1988: Short cardinal song at about eight o'clock this morning. The pre-dawn songs ended about a week ago. At South Glen, wingstem late full, ironweed, sundrops, and ironweed full, bees everywhere. Acorns now full size, most still green.

1990: Cardinals quiet most of the day. Buckeye leaves turning very quickly. Fogs moving in, humidity higher, making morning temperatures seem sharper, even though they've stayed in the 60s.

1992: Hurricane Andrew moving through Louisiana this morning. Should reach Yellow Springs in a couple of days. Cardinals quiet today, crows come and go. The first puffball mushrooms noticed growing in the woods at Grinnell and Wilberforce-Clifton Road. Crickets keep singing. Cicadas quiet until mid morning. The last firefly a few nights ago. Phlox suddenly almost gone. Redbuds and hackberry yellowing.

1993: Geese flew over at 8:45 a.m. The very last balloon flower bloomed today. Some phlox left, maybe a fourth. Daddy longlegs increasing in the house in the past week. Goldenrod has started at South Glen and Wilberforce. Two fireflies seen in half an hour of watching tonight.

1998: Honeysuckle berries turning orange, Japanese maples turning orange, too. Cleome remains a colorful complement to the zinnias and cosmos.

1999: Cardinal sings at 5:45, then silence. Heavy fog throughout town. No frog calls for days now. Koi still active and feeding heavily in the pond.

2000: This morning near 5:00, the low whinny of a screech owl in the back locust trees.

2001: From near 6:00 this morning, the blue jays were restless and loud. Now it's nearly 7:30, and the crows and cardinals are still going strong. Yesterday, very little sound from the birds, but the weather was similar to today's.

2002: Crickets were still singing when I went outside at 5:00 a.m. Doves started at 5:22, cardinals at 5:29, crows at 5:42, cricket sound diminishing as the sky lightened. The yard mostly quiet by 5:55.

2003: Three monarchs seen today.

2004: Birds becoming more common on the phone wires along Dayton-Yellow Springs Road.

2006: A cardinal sang at 5:40. A skunk wandered across the backyard around sunrise. Monarchs and skippers and swallowtails were common throughout the day. Storms tonight put an end to the late-summer drought.

2008: No birds heard this morning, but squirrels were whining at about 6:30. There was a light breeze, temperature in the high 50s, felt like Minnesota June, Yellow Springs autumn. By full daylight, the gold finches began to swarm around their feeder bags, males and females, up to eight or more at a time. In the alley, the tall coneflowers are half done. I noticed in Frank's yard for the first time his pear tree loaded with pears. At Moya's, one jumpseed is soft with white blossoms. In the church alley, a Japanese knotweed plant is full, lush. The hollyhock garden still stands, beautiful even with its blossoms gone; great mullein stalks complement the brown display.

2010: The full moon brought very cool weather to the August 25th high-pressure system, a major shift in temperature for this hot summer. In the alley, Mateo's black walnut tree is at least half bare. This morning, only faint robinsong at 5:25, and a few cardinals at 5:35. Crows far off at 5:45. On the butterfly bush, at least a dozen silver-spotted skippers at once, a female and a male tiger swallowtail, many common sulphurs, one painted lady (*Cynthia*), several monarchs. Although the number of male tiger swallowtails is dwindling, the number of sulphurs and silver-spotted skippers seems to be surging.

2012: Tropical storm Isaac strengthening and heading into the Gulf. At 9:45 this morning, a huge flock of grackles passed over the yard flying from the northwest to the southeast, settling in the trees for a few minutes then moving on, gone by 9:52. This evening at Ellis Pond: orange jewelweed and arrowhead in bloom, hickory nuts just about ripe, a few split from their hulls, most still on the trees in their green pumpkin-like outer shells. Swallowtails, a buckeye and a brown butterfly seen today.

2013: South thirty miles to Wilmington: Roadsides dominated by Jerusalem artichokes, wingstem, ironweed, knotweed, sundrops/primrose, ragweed, Queen Anne's lace, horseweed all in full bloom. Goldenrod blushing (some starting to bloom along Dayton-Yellow Springs Road), many maples turning slightly, one sweet gum with a splotch of red, an ochre shading to so much of the tree line, most soy fields deep green, but some lines of yellow in one or two.

    On the way to Fairborn later, one soybean field half turned, the earliest of all the ones I've seen so far. In the garden, one great spangled fritillary, one yellow tiger swallowtail seen. The male finches at the feeder this afternoon seemed less brilliant than they did earlier in the summer - maybe the change in sunlight, maybe an actual change in their feathers. In the alley, bittersweet berries are fat but still green. In front of the house, honeysuckle berries are dusky red, one actually bright red.

2014: A spicebush swallowtail visited the circle garden zinnias as I had coffee and a chocolate chip cookie on the porch. The butterflies continue to come, fewer than many years, but at least they are here. A painted lady (*Cynthia*) this afternoon. Moya's datura, moonflower, bloomed, fat-lipped and white. Horseweed early now. Tall autumn field thistles blooming along the road to Xenia.

2015: Mostly cloudy, cool in the middle 50s, crickets loud, buzzing, chirping, whistling: At 5:38 a.m., first the "chit" of cardinal, then the first crow, then the first melodious call of the male cardinal, then intermittent calls. Then at 5:49, a large, screaming "V" of geese flew over High Street, heading west-southwest. Goldfinches chittered as I did tai chi a little after dawn. At full daylight: the rhythmic chirps of the sparrows.

2016: Warm, muggy, humidity high for the past several weeks, sky full of sun: the tithonias haunted by yellow and black swallowtails, a black swallowtail, a monarch.

2017: Once again, a chilly morning in the low 50s. Hurricane Harvey: landfall into the Texas coast, torrential rains and record flooding. In the garden, a monarch and a yellow tiger swallowtail.

2018: Before the storm this morning, hummingbirds feeding, one spicebush swallowtail in the zinnias, one monarch in the Joe Pye.

That it would always be summer and autumn, and you always courting me....

Thomas Hardy, *Tess of the d'Urbervilles*

August 27th
The 239th Day of the Year

In the evening there were flocks of nighthawks passing southward over the valley. The tall sunflowers stood, burning on their stalks to cold seed, by the river. And high up the birds rose into sight against the darkening clouds....

Wendell Berry

Sunrise/set: 5:58/7:15
Day's Length: 13 hours 17 minutes
Average High/Low: 82/61
Average Temperature: 71
Record High: 97 – 1948
Record Low: 43 – 1910

Weather

Highs in the 90s come 25 percent of the years, 80s fifty-five percent, 70s twenty percent. Chances of completely overcast conditions: 25 percent, for rain 35 percent. Nighttime lows are usually in the 60s, but cool 50s come two or three years in ten.

Natural Calendar

Ragweed pollen disappears along with the last of the garden phlox. The great blue lobelia, landmark of late August, is in full bloom. The year's final tier of wildflowers is budding: beggarticks, bur marigolds, asters, zigzag goldenrod. Although the morning chorus of birds is over for the year, nighthawks pass over in the night, screech owls haunt the pre-dawn woods, and cardinals, crows, doves, and blue jays sometimes call off and on at daybreak.

Daybook

1982: Still blooming at South Glen: jumpseed, leafcup, clearweed, white snakeroot, tall bellflower, wingstem, Queen Anne's lace, great and common ragweed, ironweed, goldenrod, nettles, pale and spotted touch-me-nots, horse nettle, burdock, sundrops, wild lettuce, chicory, celandine, day flowers, yellow wood sorrel, showy coneflowers, daisy fleabane, bindweed, wild petunia, Joe Pye weed (old), mock cucumber, great blue lobelia, heal-all, hog peanut. First autumn violet found.

1983: First autumn violet blooming in the path at Middle Prairie. Black walnut leaves almost all down, fruit ready. A few fireflies still out.

1985: At the mill, only the tips of the blue vervain hold. Lizard's tail dropping its foliage. Water horehound, mad-dog skullcap found. Jump seeds have started to jump, and the first aster of the year is flowering, Short's aster. A last firefly tonight.

1986: Cardinal sings steadily before dawn.

1987: Starlings chatter in the trees. Leaves seems to be turning early, maybe from the dry August.

1988: Soft cardinal songs in the morning rain.

1989: Peach leaves coming down into the dahlias, knotweed half full bloom, new mullein sprouting in the iris bed. Cardinal sings at dawn and then near sundown, wistful. Ragweed turning. Yard maples falling. New sprouts of some wildflower by the peonies. Cicadas still loud near sundown. Clusters of hops, box elder weathering. At Caesar Creek, lotus and arrowhead are still in full bloom.

1990: Hundreds of yellow sulphurs swarm along Wilberforce-Clifton road.

1991: Janet Hackett called yesterday to say the katydids had stopped singing. She wondered if they had moved, been eaten, driven off by predators. Tonight when I went outside, the katydids were quiet, but then up the block they were chanting full force. Janet's insects must have just moved.

1998: A few black walnut trees in town have lost all their leaves, stand naked with their round green fruit waving in the wind. Tulip trees are a third yellow toward the college. Rapid onset of color now, cottonwoods turning all at once.

2001: I came outside at 5:35 this morning: No cardinals heard, but doves were calling. At 5:39, the bell call of a blue jay, then responses from other jays. Then crows a minute later. Finally at 5:42, a cardinal. A robin clucking at 5:45. Then scattered repetitions throughout my walk.

2002: One spicebush swallowtail, so bright blue, and a beautiful golden sulfur, the "common" sulfur.

2003: Cloudy, humid and 75 degrees at 5:00 a.m. No birds heard this morning, but the cicadas started right in with sunup. Two monarchs seen, even though I spent most of the day indoors. A violent storm this afternoon brought down a huge limb from the back locust tree. It crushed some of the north garden's zinnias and the new hydrangea.

2005: Crickets were still singing when I went outside at 5:00 a.m. Doves started at 5:22, cardinals at 5:29, crows at 5:42, crickets quieting as the sky lightened. The yard silent by 5:55.

  At South Glen, milkweed pods fully developed, milkweed bugs still mating. All the white vervain is gone. Only one or two blossoms on the small-flowered agrimony. Golden patches of linden along the roadsides. Honeysuckle berries orange, one tall goldenrod plant opening. First autumn violet blooming in the path beyond the barn. Lizard's tail dropping its foliage into Yellow Springs Creek, damselflies hunting in the pink smartweed. Burdock forming burs, Joe Pye weed almost all brown, knotweed just beginning to bloom, wild cucumber fruits an inch long. Jumpseeds have started to jump, and the first aster of the year is open.

  Tulip trees are yellowing at the college, cottonwoods turning all at once, elms and catalpas, hackberries blanching, some Virginia creeper leaves deep red on the path, some black walnut and buckeye trees almost bare. Locust leaves all over the parking lot at school. Some ash and maple foliage blushing.

A long flock of blackbirds flew over Beavercreek when I was there this morning. Starlings filled the telephone lines in Xenia, and hundreds of yellow sulphurs swarmed along Wilberforce-Clifton road this afternoon.

At home, peach leaves drift down into the dahlias, knotweed half in bloom, new mullein sprouting in the iris bed, virgin's bower opening on the trellis, stonecrop coming into bloom by the front porch. Dragonflies still hunt at the pond. New England aster buds are purple by the north trellis. Fireflies and Japanese beetles almost gone, chigger bites still itching on my right calf and ankle.

2006: Cardinal at 5:40 a.m. Bright blue morning glories have spread through the raspberries and the compost bin in the alley. Ragweed still has golden pollen. One cottonwood along Dayton-Yellow Springs Road shedding in the breeze. The honeysuckle berries at the front trellis, the markers of winter and spring for the next six months, are just beginning to turn. At the same time, a blush is forming on the bittersweet berries above the sidewalk at the corner of High and Limestone Streets.

2007: Grounding in just what lies around me, learning to understand home, learning the limits of independence, the solitude of landscape, finding enough in the most simple observations and events, embracing the ordinary and expecting nothing more, accepting this particular passage of time and location in time, seeing salvation in the commonplace, the measurement of a dragon fly, the measurement of goldenrod, asking nothing more than these plain acts, allowing, opening, watching the finite visions that contain no transcendence or special compensation, considering the precision of each fragment that names the exact place of Earth's orbit and my exact place within it now.

2008: Tropical Storm/Hurricane Fay has pounded Haiti in the past 24 hours, will head out into the Gulf today or tomorrow. Projections have it striking near New Orleans, around the three-year anniversary of Hurricane Katrina's destruction of that city. In the alley, the last of Mrs. Timberlake's late, orange day lilies is gone. The Japanese maple in Katy's yard is now yellow orange, and the bittersweet vine at Limestone Street is flushed orange. As Jeanie and I sat and read the mail after lunch, one very loud field cricket chirped and chirped.

2009: Ragweed pollen is gone in the alley as Don's goldenrod follows Mateo's. Rose hips red, prickly sow thistles bright yellow. Peggy's New England asters are blooming. A baby sparrow being fed in the back white mulberry tree. Honeysuckle berries, orange and red, stand out in the back yard. No swallowtails or monarchs seen today. This evening at 6:20, Mary Donahoe called, was watching a flock of nighthawks swooping and diving, eating insects.

2010: Hummingbird moths, common for the past month at the butterfly bush, have suddenly stopped coming to the circle garden.

2011: Cardinal at 5:35 this morning, crows at 5:45, then more cardinals, then quiet. One spicebush, one red admiral at the bushes this noon. Hummingbirds still here feeding.

2012: Light rain in the middle of the day, then after the sun came out, a few swallowtail sightings, including one giant swallowtail. Along the road to Xenia, ash, box elder and locust leaf turn is accelerating. More black walnut trees are bare. The prairie dock is still in full bloom at the south end of High Street. Peaches continue to fall, windfall apples in the alley. Suddenly the soybean fields are turning in the county and the first corn has been cut for silage. Peggy's virgin's bower has about five white blossoms, the first of the season. Bright finches continue to feed heavily. Hurricane Isaac spins toward New Orleans tonight.

2013: The first white aster has started blooming along shore of Ellis Pond. A dove was calling there this evening.

2014: The shed orb-weaver still waiting. I saw a spicebush swallowtail and a male tiger swallowtail on my walk with Bella this morning, cicadas screaming in the heat. A monarch, a great spangled fritillary and a smaller fritillary in the afternoon and then another tiger. Along the north garden, the phlox are on their last flower, and the last spiderwort shows a little violet among its blackened foliage. Now the red amaranth stands out against the late Joe Pye; the Knockout roses vie with the drifts of zinnias, and the castor beans (one six, the other ten-feet tall) frame the zinnia blossoms with their fat, red stalks and flappy, giant green leaves.

2015: Mild and partly cloudy: The crows waited until 5:38 this morning, and the first cardinal called at 5:52. A monarch and a yellow swallowtail seen today in a walk around the yard. The shed orb-weaver is at the door every morning now. A few tall goldenrod plants coming in along the road to Fairborn. One jumpseed plant was brittle enough to pop a first seed.

2016: Jill passed through an orb-weaver web on her way out the door yesterday; the spider rode home with her on her sleeve. She brushed it off in the house, and it hid under the kitchen stove. When she got out of bed, she almost walked into the huge circular web with which the orb-weaver had blocked the door between her kitchen and dining area. As she walked down High Street in the dark this morning. she heard the soft whinny of a screech owl. I found a monarch and a yellow swallowtail in the flowers when I stepped outside this afternoon. This evening, John Blakelock called to say he had seen four nighthawks on the wing – about the same time at the same day that Mary reported nighthawks in 2009.

2017: Hurricane Harvey floods Houston. Southern Texas is a disaster zone. In Madison, Wisconsin, Tat says she is seeing the first red leaves, the sky is gray and the temperature is 65.

2018: This morning, sun coming through the honeysuckles at around 7:30, a monarch is moving already, and two orb-weavers wait in their broad, sparkling webs in the north garden – one spider in the ferns, the other in a castor bean plant. Looking back over the daybook entries for this time of year, I noticed how orb-weavers and hurricanes are two sides of a Late Summer coin. A pair of mating monarchs this afternoon, a giant swallowtail, a spicebush swallowtail and a great spangled fritillary in the zinnias. The

Japanese knotweed branches are heavy with blossoms and full of bees. Above the back porch, the trumpet creeper no longer blooms, sports long, green seed pods.

A vast similitude interlocks all,
All spheres, grown, ungrown, small, large, suns,
moons, planets..

Walt Whitman

August 28th
The 240th Day of the Year

The rayons of the sun we see
Diminish in their strength,
The shade of every tower and tree
Extended is in length.

Alexander Hume

Sunrise/set: 5:59/7:13
Day's Length: 13 hours 14 minutes
Average High/Low: 82/61
Average Temperature: 71
Record High: 96 – 1953
Record Low: 40 – 1910

Weather

Today is another pivot day on the way to autumn as the chances of a high in the 60s rise to 15 percent. Seventy-degree highs take place 25 percent of the time; 80s occur 40 percent, 90s twenty percent. Lows dip below 60 on a third of all the nights. Rain falls (and the sun fails to shine) today 65 percent of the years, making this is one of the three wettest and grayest days of the summer months; July 3rd and June 20th are the other two. And, for the first time since the beginning of June, the lightest of frosts becomes a slight possibility.

Natural Calendar

It is the week of the first frost in the Montana mountains, time for snow in Canada. Sundogs, sun through crystals, sometimes form over the Ohio Valley these afternoons, foretaste of the winter sky.

Daybook

1979: Northeast maple in the yard starts to turn.

1981: All lightning bugs gone.

1982: Geese fly over 7:45 a.m. All lightning bugs gone. Raspberries continue to come in, another quart this morning.

1983: Down the railroad tracks past the Vale: Hops in layered flowers, catmint still in bloom, tall bellflower fading. Dayflowers, ironweed, jumpseed, smartweed, giant yellow hyssop, white morning glories, a few domestic phlox holding. Field thistle up to seven feet with bright violet flowers. Wild cherry has dark fruit. Purple berries and fading leaves on the pokeweed. Sundrops remain, but most great mulleins gone. White sweet clover hanging on, probably cut over. Thin-leafed coneflowers late bloom, boneset and white snakeroot still common. Elms seem to be getting lighter, blanching with the approach of fall. Milkweed bugs are still mating, spotted orange touch-me-nots still blooming, wingstem, a few fleabane, beggarticks almost blooming, soapwort, goldenrod not even yellow here; horseweed, burdock brown and bent. Trumpet creepers still strong, bright orange.

1984: The leaves are turning: catalpas are paling, some maples red, some yellowing. Poplars, hackberries started to deteriorate a week or two ago.

1988: Now elderberries are deep purple (as are my grapes) and sweet for picking. *Rudbeckia speciosa*, showy coneflower, still full bloom, but shifting past its peak. Japanese knotweed open in the yard. Milkweed bugs still mating.

1989: Mourning doves still calling off and on today, Late Summer holding.

1990: More cabbage butterflies along Wilberforce-Clifton. Some great autumnal hatch.

1992: Joe Pye weed at Wilberforce still full bloom. Doves call after dawn. Cardinals sing once, 5:45 a.m. Last of the white phlox today; several red blossoms stay. Goldenrod finally blooms along Grinnell and throughout my drive. Monarchs and swallowtails increasing at the zinnias.

1998: Tulip trees half yellow. The pond's last arrowhead bloomed today; the rest of the plant has round and green seedpods, three-fourths of an inch across. Some black walnut trees in town are completely bare, fruits dangling in the wind.

1999: A dove was calling this morning, maybe eight o'clock. Some goldenrod flushed but not even close to opening. Heliopsis and showy coneflowers continue to deteriorate quickly, the south garden finally losing its vitality. Along the Carolina coast, Hurricane Dennis is moving in.

2000: Soft whinny of a screech owl in the back trees at 6:13 a.m.

2001: Only crickets this morning until one cardinal sang at 5:45. Webworms noticed in the pussy willows. They must have just emerged – their web seeming to appear over night. Scorpion fly found in the north garden.

2002: Two monarchs flew by together as I walked near the zinnias. This afternoon, I found an ailanthus webworm moth on the archway into the house.

2003: Fall sedum is coming into bloom by the front porch. Four more monarchs seen today. A huge camel cricket got into the tub last night, was hiding behind the shampoo bottles this morning. Bella found a baby squirrel among the debris of the locust that fell yesterday. It was three to four weeks old, eyes not open yet. We gave it a little liquid, then took it to an animal rescue center in Troy.

2004: One cardinal song at 5:50 this morning. A flock of crows was calling about five minutes later. Then silence, then more crows and cardinals a little after 6:00, then quiet. Working outside this afternoon, I noticed how sluggish the scorpion flies were, allowing me to brush them off the plants.

2005: Doves calling at 5:30 a.m. Cardinals a little later. At Antioch School, the mountain maple seeds hang in brown clusters.

2007: Heat and clear sky today before the cool front due tomorrow. Japanese knotweed, stonecrop, jumpseeds, Queen Anne's lace, black-eyed Susans, a few roses, hibiscus and the Royal Standard hosta are the perennials flowering in the yard. Rose of Sharon blossoms are becoming scarce. Few birds have come to the feeder the past day or two, almost no morning birdsong. Painted lady (*Cynthia*) butterfly seen in the garden yesterday and the day before – the first I've noticed this summer. I drove south to Hillsboro this evening. Once I reached Jamestown about 15 miles from home, I reached the drought area. From there for the next 40 miles, the corn fields were stressed and withering, soybeans stunted and turning gold. The grass on one graveyard was completely brown.

2008: Silent mornings, thunderous katydids at night. The finches, males still very bright gold, continue to feed hard. No monarch butterflies since the 18th. More streaks of yellow in the black walnut trees along Limestone Street. Red maple foliage has faded at the triangle park. Hawthorn berries still green, the pollen berries still holding. The alley is on the edge of Early Fall, only the great mullein pollen keeping it in summer. Against the stone wall, white and red Oriental lilies have come into bloom from a late planting. This evening, well before dark, a large black skunk with white top fur scrounged for sunflower seeds under the bird feeders in the back yard.

2009: Hops clusters heavy on the honeysuckles. Heliopsis, black-eyed Susans, Shasta daisies, *Rudbeckia speciosa* hold. Late giant hibiscus, a handful of pink mallow, strong Knock-out roses. Full knotweed, ironweed about gone, late hostas still strong, dahlias, butterfly bushes. Oakleaf hydrangeas still provide body and variety to the northwest garden. Phlox are spotty but bright. Webworms high in the box elder.

2010: Skippers still abundant, monarchs, male and female tiger swallowtails still steady visitors to the butterfly bushes and zinnias.

2011: Several monarchs, one spicebush swallowtail, one buckeye, many skippers and cabbage butterflies today. No cardinal heard this morning, but a dove and crows were calling between 6:00 and 7:00. Chickadees and hummingbirds feeding back and forth around 8:00.

2012: Whistling crickets and handsome trigs at 5:00 a.m., Orion in the east, Jupiter overhead, Venus rising, crows at 5:30, a distant cardinal at 5:40, tufted titmouse at 5:45. Only crows at vespers. More trees join the color: ochre cottonwoods, yellow and orange sycamores, drooping catalpas.

2013: On the way to the airport, I saw the first great flock of starlings of the autumn swooping and diving south above the freeway.

2014: Walking with Jeff along the bike path south of Cedarville: Wingstem, bouncing bets, ironweed, early goldenrod, field thistles, white snakeroot all in bloom. One buckeye butterfly, one small black swallowtail, one monarch, one male tiger swallowtail. The berries of a bittersweet vine were pale gold, and most of the berries from a wild cherry tree had fallen to the path, as had wild cherry fruit yesterday at John Bryan Park. At home, another tiger, a frenetic great spangled fritillary, and many cabbage whites. Around the neighborhood, autumn allium, stonecrop, virgin's bower, late white-flowered hostas, late rudbeckia dominate the perennial gardens. No birdsong in the evening.

2015: Crows at 5:35. A glance outside in the sun, warm: a monarch at the tithonias. In the yard, one tall red hibiscus, one lily, a yellow rebloomer, late violet hostas with late blossoms, new September hostas reaching early bloom, jumpseeds, Shasta daisies, knotweed, rudbeckia, pink-flowered stonecrop (Autumn Joy) and the clearweed which has filled in around almost all the plants, offering a deep green groundcover.

2016: Day trip to southwest Ohio with Jill: Lush farmland throughout, some fields brown with corn tassels, only one soybean field turning. Wildflowers in the mountains: ironweed, Jerusalem artichokes, wingstem, field thistles, Joe Pye weed (less gray than the ones at home), some early goldenrod. Then as we walked in the evening before sundown, and as dark storm clouds were appearing in the northwest, Jill spotted a long, long line of blackbirds just above the eastern woods, several branches of the flock moving to join the larger group, all of them flying southeast away from the storm, their passage seeming to last forever – maybe five minutes.

2017: A cardinal sang at 5:36, crows just a few minutes later. The first Jumpseeds jump when I finger their stems. Buds have formed on some of the New England asters, but no purple shows yet. Small (perhaps recently emerged) scorpion flies, the first I have seen since spring. A very large flock of starlings (probably) flew over the grocery store when we arrived in the early evening. Heavy rain, up to 50 inches, has flooded the whole city of Houston, the worst flood in American history.

Like imaginary lines of longitude and latitude, the plats of zeitgebers (clusters of events in nature that tell the time of year) delineate space as well as time, name local as well as regional dimensions of the Earth's relationship to the Sun and provide soft borders to the seasons.

Bradford Townsend

August 29th
The 241st Day of the Year

98 years, 3 months, 2 days. Time is marching.
Been sitting on the porch listening and watching
as the sun lowers behind the horizon.
Hummingbirds first to retire,
and at dusk robins cluck the benediction for day,
and the tree frog follows with invocation for night activities
to start with wonderful sky line colors at that time.

A note from Ruby Nicholson, age 98, 3 months, 2 days,
August 29, 2008

Sunrise/set: 6:00/7:12
Day's Length: 13 hours 12 minutes
Average High/Low: 82/61
Average Temperature: 71
Record High: 96 – 1953
Record Low: 41 – 1986

Weather

Nineties comes 30 percent of the afternoons; 80s occur 30 percent of the time, 70s thirty percent, 60s ten percent. Today is typically twice as sunny as yesterday, with all but 20 percent of the days bringing clear or partly cloudy skies. Rain falls three years in ten. Another pivot to autumn, this one a bit dramatic: a very light frost could appear on the roof one year in every 25. One night in three drops below 60 degrees.

Natural Calendar

Cottonwoods are turning, and box elders, catalpas have started to lose their color. A few big yellow leaves of the white mulberry drop early. Sometimes all the black walnut leaves are down. Locusts and lindens are rusting from leafminers. The rare Judas maple of early August spreads its orange and red across the hillsides.

Daybook

1982: Record low temperatures reported in northern Minnesota and Wisconsin. Arrowhead still blooming at Ellis Pond. Geese came over the house after supper.

1984: West from Maryland to Ohio: Touch-me-nots full throughout, white and yellow moth mullein common. Sundrops everywhere, Joe Pye strong but some fading. First white asters picked, *aster pilosus*. Clovers abundant; crown vetch, yellow and white sweet clover. Old standbys of Late Summer: Queen Anne's lace, chicory, wingstem, ironweed throughout the East. Wild lettuce definitely done. Mullein and burdock are old but still blooming, milkweed gone, its leaves yellow green. Horseweed strong. Japanese knotweed here and there, some butter and eggs. Home by suppertime. Geese flew over the house at 6:30 p.m.

1986: No cardinals heard at all today.

1987: Honeybees working the goldenrod, huge yellow nodules of pollen on their legs. Cardinal sang at 9:30 and 10:00 a.m.

1988: First maple tree leaves in the yard turned over night in the rain. Wingstem fading, burdock forming burs. Common dodder (love vine) has colored the riverbanks rust with its tangle of tendrils, and is finally in bloom. At the Covered Bridge, Joe Pye weed is almost all brown, goldenrod and knotweed just opening. First woolly bear caterpillar of the year seen today. Crickets not heard tonight.

1989: Cardinals and doves began to sing a half hour before dawn. They've continued now for hours. Is it the beginning of second spring - a renewal of birdsong?

1990: Cardinal called once this morning, then quiet.

1992: My ash at Wilberforce is almost completely golden green.

1996: The wren nest in the begonia hanging on the front porch is finally empty. The mother tended the two eggs and the babies all August.

1998: Cardinal sang at 5:37 this morning, crows followed, then a wren. The birds sang off and on for half an hour or so. By 7:30, grackles and doves were calling, the others quiet. In the pond, the water lilies continue to bloom, one or two a day. The last arrowhead is flowering today, and its seedpods are big and green now, its leaves yellowing. Autumn coming quickly.

1999: Cardinals and crows this morning at about 5:40. Then quiet for a while, then a resurgence by 6:30, then more quiet.

2000: To Wilmington and back: Flurries of black walnut leaves, goldenrod in bloom, false boneset, field thistles, sundrops, tall coneflowers, Queen Anne's lace, chicory, horseweed, Jerusalem artichokes, stonecrop, jewel weed. At Wilberforce, my ash tree is losing leaves on schedule, and maybe a fourth of the leaves are yellow. On Wilberforce-Clifton road, one mimosa tree is still in bloom.

2001: Jumpseed is still in full bloom along the sidewalk in front of the house. One Judas maple turning in Hustead, but nothing else all the way to Columbus. Then: yellow locust leaves all over the parking lot at the university. From my office window at the university, one red maple has just a tinge of color here and there. The great white oak is still pure dark green.

2003: At South Glen, some buckeyes are completely bare. Wild cucumber is in full bloom, some fruits more than half an inch long. Wingstem and ironweed are still in flower, goldenrod here still just budding (although yesterday I saw several plants open along the road to Troy). A few jumpseeds are jumping, some wood nettle leaves turning white.

2004: Crickets were still singing at 5:00 this morning; they quieted in proportion to the advance of sunrise. No cardinals until 6:10, then silence until I heard doves about 6:30.

2005: Hummingbird moth seen in the impatiens at about 10:30. Monarchs still common in the zinnias.

2007: A cardinal called twice at 5:40 this morning, crows came by at 5:55. Tall coneflowers decline suddenly in the alley. Jumpseeds aren't jumping yet. A hummingbird came to the feeder off and on this morning.

2008: Hurricane Gustav points to New Orleans. The first peach fell from the home tree yesterday. Today, I noticed a pile of red windfall apples in an orchard on the way back from Fairborn. No doves calling for a few days. Sparrows and finches continue to feed heavily. Clusters of cabbage butterflies romp in the north garden. One monarch came by in the afternoon.

2010: This morning's raspberries, a full pint, seemed to be the peak of the season. Three male tiger swallowtails and numerous silver-spotted skippers in the butterfly bush while we had lunch today. Hurricanes, absent until last week this summer, are lining up in the Caribbean. Here, the grass is turning brown for lack of rain. Along the roads, the dry weather is taking its toll, blanching grasses and trees, turning the soybean fields more quickly. Knotweed is in full bloom at home and in the alley. From Spoleto, Italy, Neysa says that she and Ivano picked nine kilos of blackberries in the hills near the city.

2011: A cardinal sang at 5:38 this morning - but only continued for ten minutes or so, crows at 5:45, squirrels started at 7:00. The high grating trill of crickets when I first went outside, occasionally voiced-over by the ghostly whistling crickets. Hummingbird wars, as Jeanie calls their competing to drink from the red feeder Ruby gave us, continued through the day,. The first of Moya's jumpseed jumped when I stroked it as I walked with Bella by her house. One monarch, one black and one tiger swallowtail seen, one brown, one blue. Crickets loud at night, but katydids seem to be tapering off. One chigger bite from yesterday or this morning.

2012: Only crows this morning about 5:30. High trigs, occasional whistling crickets. Scattered birdsong later, crows, blue jays, a cardinal. Sparrows staying away from the feeder, but bright finches, up to five at a time, on the finch bags.

2013: An orb-weaver made its web on the tall bird feeder over night. A dove was calling in the back at 5:30 this morning. Small basket of peaches picked for Janie, plenty more on the tree, the windfalls holding back some. Goldenrod finally coming into bloom along the highway. Petals fallen from the winterberry flowers. A fledgling goldfinch fluttering its wings, begging for food on top of the feeder. Honeybees swarming around the hummingbird food, the hummingbirds having to push their way through to eat. Fewer swallowtails today. Tonight, whistling crickets joined the thrips at about 7:15, katydids started in at 7:35.

2014: Bright and warm. The sparrows stayed away a while: chickadees, tufted titmice, cardinals come to the feeder. Lots of cabbage whites today, two yellow tiger swallowtails, one faded and bedraggled black, and a great spangled fritillary. At the North Glen, the very first aster was opening, one white flower on what seems to be the foliage of Short's aster – leaves not toothed at all, large and shaped like elongated hearts.

2015: Crows at 5:44 this morning, one cardinal chipping, then trying to warm up at 5:38, then silence. No doves calling or even sparrows chirping. One monarch seen – a quiet day for butterflies. In the Women's Park, all the heliopsis and coneflowers are gone. Only some early white asters are in bloom, and the cup plant. The High Street prairie dock continues full bloom. Along Dayton Street, a few maples are turning. In the late afternoon, I sat on the porch, the wind before the coming storm pulled showers of yellow locust leaves to the yard beside me. Tonight, the crickets and katydids are in full song as the storm draws nearer.

2016: I noticed a hummingbird moth in the zinnias this morning, the first one I've seen since early July when the monarda was in full bloom.

2017: A small black swallowtail and a pipevine swallowtail in the zinnias at noon. In Texas: the greatest amount of rainfall with one event in American history. This is also the anniversary of the landfall of Hurricane Katrina in New Orleans in 2005. The last days of August: the crucible of Global Warming in the Atlantic Ocean.

2018: Inventory in the yard, sun, humid and still and very warm: Jeanie's ancient yellow tea rose bloomed yesterday; two blossoms on the Knockout rose that was burned back by frost two years ago; two new Shasta daisy blossoms (but that is all the daisies): Joe Pye gray but bright ironweed behind them; fragments of daisy fleabane near the northwest corner of the property; phlox holding on; most ferns withered; hackberry tree half down, leaves shriveling; Royal Standard hostas late full: violet-flowered thin-leaf hostas full; milkweed pods fat and sticky, milkweed foliage curled with age; honeysuckle berries dusky red; slightly blushing bittersweet berries; pokeweed berries mostly green, a few purple; two late Annabelle hydrangea blossoms; late rose of Sharon flowers; trumpet creeper mostly to seed pods, the golden-flowered ones in front still have a few blooms; stonecrop opening steadily; the tall decorative grass seeding; blue day flowers open; purple coneflowers withered or colorless; knotweed full and heavy with bees; jumpseed mostly gone; only about a dozen heliopsis flowers left; zinnias and tithonia and castor beans full bloom, many dahlias and a few canna lilies giving most of the brightness to the yard; New England asters lanky almost budding; lily foliage streaked with decayed leaves; rusty blush on the viburnum; Jeanie's river birch foliage yellowing; monarchs, silver spotted skippers and cabbage whites always here, occasionally a spicebush swallowtail, a male tiger swallowtail., small, golden fold-wing skippers.

Not the sun or the summer alone, but every hour and season yields its tribute of delight; for every hour and change corresponds to and authorizes a different state of the mind.

Ralph Waldo Emerson

August 30th
The 242nd Day of the Year

Everywhere in the countryside there is a glimmer of autumn reds. Hawthorn bushes are laden with crimson berries, while the clusters of black elderberries are surrounded with vinous red leaves. On brambles, the ripening berries are a glossy purple and some of the leaves are scarlet. The lower leaves of docks are also turning bright red.

Derwent May

Sunrise/set: 6:01/7:10
Day's Length: 13 hours 9 minutes
Average High/Low: 81/60
Average Temperature: 71
Record High: 96 – 1953
Record Low: 43 – 1986

Weather
Today is mild in the 70s fifty percent of the time; there is a 40 percent chance of 80s, ten percent for 90s. Rain, along with a totally or mostly cloudy day, comes one year out of three. Four nights in twelve dip below 60 degrees.

Natural Calendar
Crickets, katydids and cicadas are still loud as stonecrop reaches early bloom. Along the lakeshores, arrowhead is declining rapidly, lotus weakening. Telephone wires fill with birds as migrations accelerate. Orb-weavers weave their webs for September. Quince fruits fall from their branches in the night.

Daybook
1983: Some maple leaves falling in South Glen. Cabbage butterflies still mating. Geese flew over in the evening.

1988: Geese flew over this evening, eight o'clock. Pennsylvania leatherwings mating on the knotweed flowers.

1989: Cardinals, crows, doves began to sing near dawn. As I got up, a robin gave a long, loud call that lasted maybe half a minute, like a valediction to summer.

1990: At South Glen, some wingstem and ironweed have started to go to seed. Coneflowers and helianthus still in bloom. The tree line is rusting now, so much deepening of color, wearing down, decaying. Goldenrod just starting at South Glen, one or two heads open here and there. Zigzag goldenrod is budding under the canopy. Blue cohosh berries are thinning, red clusters of Jack-in-the-pulpit have toppled. Wood nettle has gone to seed, ragweed old now.

1996: A short stop at South Glen: butterflies everywhere, so many species. The woods and undergrowth tattered now, leaves turning early. Goldenrod just coming in. At home, the pink asters (the annuals grown from seed) are full and strong. The zinnias continue to bloom well, but the cosmos are falling over. The ladyslippers have completely disappeared in the past week, and the showy coneflowers are at least half gone.

1998: The fish in the pond have been quieter, more reluctant to rise over the past two weeks. Water and sky clear, season of clarity.

2001: No birdsong this morning until a dove started singing at 5:37. A few minutes later crows, then a jay. No cardinals until after sunrise. Rhythms changing, syncopating.

2002: Knotweed full bloom in the yard. First woolly bear caterpillar seen on the other side of the butterfly preserve. Wingstem prominent, ironweed almost all gone. Red berries on the Jack-in-the-pulpit. A large brown wood nymph seen, like a *Satyrus pagala* in the blackberry bushes.

2003: Two monarchs in the garden today in the hour or so that I was outside. Birds flocking – look like starlings – on the wires when we drove to Dayton this morning.

2004: A long flock of blackbirds flew over Beavercreek when I was there this morning at 9:30. All across the city, ashes are turning quickly. Along Dayton Street, the serviceberry trees have lost almost all their leaves. No bird song this morning, not even a crow. Casey told me that when he and Rusty Neff, Joe Ayers and Eli Sweatland were having coffee at Dino's, they talked about the unusually intense activity of the squirrels. "They were packing walnuts like they were just invented," said Casey. "Looks like it's going to be a cold winter."

2005: The rain from Hurricane Katrina is reaching Yellow Springs today, 24 hours after it struck New Orleans. The rain will nurture the new lettuce that just sprouted by the tomatoes in the garden. Cardinals and doves were quiet this morning, and the crickets stopped calling by 6:00 a.m. Albert, the pond's green frog, croaked once at about 6:45 a.m. Arrowhead still open in the water garden.

2006: Cardinal at 5:45 a.m. Mateo's goldenrod is about a half in bloom. The goldenrod at the Dayton Street side of the alley is still just starting to show some color. No doves heard lately.

2007: Four hummingbirds noticed together in the garden this noon – a small migrating group? Cabbage butterflies abundant.

2008: Windfall apples increasing in the alley, the tree's branches straining under the fruit, one branch broken. Our peach tree also shows the weight of fully developed fruit. No bird calls early this morning, but the white-headed skunk came by at about 6:00, and sparrow and finch feeding began at 6:30. One giant swallowtail, one tiger swallowtail in the back yard at about 10:00 a.m. One monarch seen in the front garden about 12:00 p.m., two more late in the afternoon.

2009: To western Michigan. Three monarchs, starling flocks throughout – one very large. Goldenrod along the roadsides and golden corn tassels. Huge white datura at a rest stop. At the dunes: knapweed, clustered and tall goldenrod, a few small white asters, very late white sweet clover. Habitat of sassafras, witch hazel, cottonwood, ash, red maple, sumac.

2010: Robins at 5:30, crows at 5:45, a few cardinal songs at 6:00. Swallowtails (male tiger and spicebush) still visit the butterfly bushes, silver-spotted skippers swarm still, peaches continue to fall (more than three-fourths down now, and sweeter). No monarchs seen today. Five flowering cabbage plants set out in the dooryard garden, six mums along the north garden's edge. No robin vespers noticed tonight.

2011: No cardinals this morning, but a robin heard peeping in the back bushes, and crows passing through west of town. Temperature in the low 50s when I got up, the tree crickets faint for the first time since the beginning of the month. Chickadees, cardinals (giving only their brief, sharp call note) and hummingbirds at the feeders. Sparrows not as common as two weeks ago, their consumption of seeds suddenly way down. When I walked Bella around 7:00 this evening, the tree crickets were gaining energy, and a few field crickets were singing.

2012: No early birdsong heard, only trigs and whistling crickets. Katydids still rasping at night. An abundance of smaller butterflies today.

2013: One male tiger and two Eastern Black swallowtails in the zinnias today, only one skipper, no hummingbird moths, a decline in numbers and species. The Knockout roses are now coming back and providing color to the north garden, the dead-heading and pruning of a month ago producing results. Dahlias strong, Shasta daisies strong, butterfly bushes holding, zinnias dominant. Peaches maybe a fourth fallen or picked.

2014: The shed orb-weaver is still waiting at its web. Cardinals heard around 5:45 this morning, the male's song, but mostly the "chit-chit" of the female. A squirrel joined them before 6:00. Jays called after dawn. Cicadas started at exactly 7:14. Throughout the day, dozens of white cabbage butterflies playing and spinning, several tiger swallowtails and painted ladies, one giant swallowtail.

2015: Goldenrod outside of town is solid gold in some fields. At my pond, the first flower of the swamp beggarticks was open this morning, the standard beggarticks still just budded. At the yellow spring, lush wingstem, touch-me-nots, white snakeroot. The shed orb-weaver remained impassive in his web as I chiseled niches for hinges to the door.

2016: Sunny and warm. Many silver-spotted skippers, fold-wing skippers, one black swallowtail (with some blue on tail, most likely a pipevine), one great spangled fritillary, one tiger swallowtail. Another long flock of blackbirds seen today, this one flying right over town. Many leaves from the backyard cherry tree when I mowed the lawn this afternoon. More maples have become tinged with rust and orange. In the night, quince fruits have been falling on the tin roof of the bedroom – perhaps for a week?

2017: Bright sun and mild No quince fruits noticed this year. One monarch flew across the zinnia gardens at about 9:00 this morning. He stayed for an hour or so exploring. After lunch, a painted lady. At South Glen, full bloom of wild cucumbers and yellow touch-me-not, aging tall bellflowers, early white snakeroot, wood nettle to seed, full boneset and wingstem, burdock done with berries still green, some of the jumpseed jumping. And as I made my way along the overgrown pathways, I walked through micrathena webs every ten paces or so, finally giving up after breaking up dozens of spider barriers.

2018: To Allegheny State Park in western New York State: some soybean fields turning, pacing the blushing goldenrod beside them. Pale horseweed leans in the wind. At the park, small white asters starting, late Queen Anne's lace, jewelweed, boneset, Jerusalem artichokes, chicory, hawkweed, masses of knotweed, sow thistles, purple loosestrife, a new rough-leafed aster with alternate, toothed leaves not clasping, hard stem, white flowers with six to eight petals with yellow centers, occasional New England asters,

> *The Beauty which old Greece or Rome*
> *Sang, painted, wrought, lies here at home;*
> *We need but eye and ear*
> *In all our daily walks to trace*
> *The outlines of incarnate grace,*
> *The hymns of gods to hear.*

John Greenleaf Whittier

August 31st
The 243rd Day of the Year

What means this sense of lateness that so comes over one now, -- as if the rest of the year were down-hill. The night of the year is approaching. What have we done with our talent? All nature prompts and reproves us. How early in the year it begins to be late!

Henry David Thoreau

Sunrise/set: 6:02/7:09
Day's Length: 13 hours 7 minutes
Average High/Low: 81/60
Average Temperature: 71
Record High: 100 – 1951
Record Low: 42 – 1915

Weather

Forty percent of the early morning temperatures are in the 50s today. Highs climb to 90 ten percent of the afternoons, to the 80s fifty percent, and the 70s forty percent. The chance of rain continues to be about 35 percent. A totally cloudy day occurs this last day of the month five years in a dozen.

Natural Calendar

Deep in the woods, the final days of the year's wildflowers coincide with the first days of second spring, which are actually the first days of next spring. March's purple deadnettle comes up in the garden. The garlic mustard that will flower two Aprils from now sprouts in the rain. Wood mint produces new stalks. Watercress revives in the sloughs. Next May's sweet rockets and next July's avens send up fresh basal leaves. Sweet Cicely foliage grows back. Sedum reappears, stalky from its canopied summer.

Daybook

1983: Goldenrod turning slowly now.

1984: Velvetleaf going to seed in the yellowing soybeans here, but stronger as I went north to Wisconsin.

1986: No cardinals heard today. Ragweed pollen gone in the yard. Soybean leaves half yellow. Some ash foliage reddening.

1987: Cardinals singing sporadically near 7:00 this morning, then quiet. Maple in front of the house is starting to turn.

1989: Now a rapid turning of leaves, some Osage yellow, and the lower leaves of the tree of heaven are turning. No more fireflies, no cardinals, no doves. Crickets, katydids and cicadas still loud. Prime of the last full wildflower bloom. At Caesar Creek, catfish have disappeared from my fishing hole, replaced by yellow bullheads. Along the shore, arrowhead is declining rapidly, lotus weakening.

1996: Mill Habitat with Rainer to check water quality of the Little Miami: We found a large turtle sleeping in the riffle, counted a number of Dobson fly larvae, caddis fly larvae, beetle larvae, found a Mayfly larva, a small red water worm, and a small live clam. The water quality was fair to good, according to the standards Rainer has been using.

1997: The days have been mild. Yellow patches on the silver olives. Virginia creeper reddening. Resurrection lilies all gone. Large sedum in full bloom.

1999: South Glen: Goldenrod shows plenty of color in Duckwall's fields. Under the canopy, the first zigzag goldenrod is opening. Jumpseeds are still soft, not jumping at all. The small white asters are budding, but not really close to opening. Garlic mustard for 2001 has sprouted from the last rain (a week ago). At home, the maple shows orange patches, and the ash at the southeast corner of the yard is yellowing. Ironweed is starting its down side. Along the bike path, all the coneflowers are dying back at once.

2000: Rudbeckia and ironweed are dying back quickly now, and the very last of the arrowhead is in bloom. Birds fill the telephone wires at the market. Showers of apple, locust and black walnut leaves fall in the sultry 90-degree afternoon. I found toads an inch long in the grass.

2003: Cardinals and doves heard at 5:50 in the cool, rainy morning, still singing at 6:30 when I started breakfast.

2004: A chilly, quiet morning, few crickets before dawn. A few chigger bites remain on my right calf and ankle.

2006: Chiggers continue to bite Jeanie when she works outside in the garden. Large orb-weaver spiders spinning evening webs from the porch beams. In the northwest garden, ironweed, the pink rose, heliopsis, a few zinnias, and several large clumps of black-eyed Susans keep color in the yard. Pink sedum in the east garden is half in flower. Virgin's bower well budded on our trellis, but in full bloom at the corner of Elm and Dayton Streets.

2007: Chiggers seem to be coming back with drier weather. One Japanese beetle found in the roses today. No birds heard before sunrise. Pink sedum in the east garden is half in flower. Two more hummingbirds seen together today. No fireflies seen for at least a week or two. Don's showy coneflowers are at least half decayed.

2008: Faint crows and doves around 5:50 a.m., then silence. I noticed the finches feeding at 6:10. Sparrows and finches flock in the yard through the day. Starlings clucking in the trees when I walked Bella at 9:00, continuing to whistle and cluck into the afternoon.

2009: Central western Michigan, Silver Lake State Park: One monarch. Joe Pye weed full and pink, purple loosestrife, hollyhocks, chicory common. One moth mullein seen. Rudbeckia and mums in the gardens. Mother and three baby ducks feeding at dusk. Horsemint in the dunes, wood mint with red stems and tufted flower tops along Silver Lake. One late daylily and a little daisy fleabane at the campsite. Large flying ants struggling to maneuver in the sand of the huge, rolling dunes.

2010: Locusts, box elders, ashes, walnuts, cottonwoods weathering more rapidly, some maples, too. At the drugstore, Marge talked about how many butterflies had come to their butterfly bushes all summer. She had never seen so many swallowtails.

2011: Very quiet at 5:30 this morning, only crows heard at 5:50, high, harsh trill of tree crickets. Bees and skippers and cabbage butterflies, one hummingbird moth at the flowers today, but no other butterflies seen. Goldenrod is blushing along the highway, and the first plants are blooming along Fairfield Pike. In the garden, four buds of false boneset have opened. As I was clipping the bushes today, a gold-bodied tree cricket jumped out of the foliage onto my arm, probably a "handsome trig."

2012: No morning bird song heard. Dry conditions contributing to rapid leaf turn. At Lawson Place, the cottonwood is shedding, and the serviceberry trees along Dayton Street are weathering quickly. The box elder is losing leaves at the park. The raspberries, when I can find them, are small and few, the leaves drooping. In all, a pale, dry garden landscape, overgrown with crabgrass. Most of the peaches have fallen now, the phlox and the Shasta daisies have ended their seasons. Showy coneflowers at Peggy's yard have suddenly withered, and ours are going fast.

2013: Doves heard after sunrise this morning. A large orb-weaver found in its web in the front shrubs. Honeysuckle bushes downtown have red berries. Peggy's showy coneflowers are drooping. Three large soybean fields on the way to Fairborn have turned in the last few days.

2014: The rose of Sharon is gone except for just a few scattered blossoms. All of Peggy's gray-headed coneflowers have withered, and all of our Joe Pye flowers have gone to seed. The soybean fields north of town are turning yellow. The showy coneflowers hold strong in town, as does the black walnut foliage. The orb-weaver on my shed door ran when it saw me coming – when I was still maybe twenty feet away.

2015: Only two rose of Sharon blossoms left in my yard and Moya's. Peggy's autumn allium and virgin's bower fill the south side of her house, showy coneflowers the front. Across from the covered bridge, the swamp is filled with full boneset and spotted touch-me-nots (*Impatiens capensis*).

2016: Skippers – fold-wing silver-spotted – dominate the butterfly populations, but two Eastern black swallowtails seen, and even a hummingbird moth, the second this week.

2017: A painted lady butterfly in the garden at 8:30 this morning, the grass and flowers wet with dew. The lady stayed throughout the day, it seems. A silver-spotted skipper and an azure were the only other butterflies. Jill saw a monarch and a sizeable flock of starlings ("the biggest murmurations I've seen so far.") on her way home from Delaware, Ohio. At Clifton Gorge, asters buds prominent, the first zigzag goldenrod open.

In the least
As well as in the greatest of His works
Is ever manifest his presence kind;
As well in swarms of glittering insects, seen
Quick to and from within a foot of air,
Dancing a merry hour, then seen no more,
As in the systems of resplendent worlds,
Through time revolving in unbound space.

Carlos Wilcox

Bill Felker has been writing *Poor Will's Almanack* for newspapers and magazines since 1984, and he has published annual almanacs since 2003. His radio version of *Poor Will* is a weekly feature on WYSO, a National Public Radio station, and is available on podcast at **www.wyso.org.** His annual almanacks, his first book of essays, *Home is the Prime Meridian: Essays in Search of Time and Place and Spirit,* and the entire twelve volumes of *A Daybook for the Year in Yellow Springs, Ohio,* can be purchased on Amazon.

For more information, visit Bill Felker's website at **www.poorwillsalmanack.com**

Made in the USA
Lexington, KY
06 August 2019